Managing Organizational Knowledge

ASTD
LEARNING
SYSTEM

Module 8

ASTD

PRESS

ASTD Press is an internationally renowned source of insightful and practical information on workplace learning and performance topics, including training basics, evaluation and return-on-investment (ROI), instructional systems development (ISD), e-learning, leadership, and career development.

Ordering information: The *ASTD Learning System* and other books published by ASTD Press can be purchased by visiting our Website at store.astd.org or by calling 800.628.2783 or 703.683.8100.

Library of Congress Control Number: 2006920963

ISBN-10: 1-56286-446-7

ISBN-13: 978-1-56286-446-0

ASTD Press Staff
Director: Cat Russo
Manager, Acquisitions and Author Relations: Mark Morrow
Editorial Manager: Jacqueline Edlund-Braun
Deputy Editor: Jennifer Mitchell
Sr. Associate Editor: Tora Estep
Circulation Manager: Marnee Beck
Editorial Assistant: Maureen Soyars
Production Coordinator: Glenn Saltzman
Cover Design: Alizah Epstein

Composition by Stephen McDougal, Mechanicsville, Maryland, www.alphawebtech.net
Printed by Victor Graphics, Baltimore, Maryland, www.victorgraphics.com.

Contents

Note: To ensure optimal instructional design in this module, the order of some Key Knowledge areas has been changed from the *Early Bird Guide to ASTD Professional Certification* (2005). These changes do not affect the integrity of the content.

Introduction

Collecting, storing, and sharing knowledge and information is crucial to the success of organizations. Training is a component of knowledge management; the sharing of information through instruction. However, there is a range of understanding required to create a successful, comprehensive knowledge-sharing environment. The workplace learning and performance professional has a responsibility to initiate, drive, and integrate knowledge management efforts within his or her organization.

The authors of the *ASTD Competency Study: Mapping the Future* defined key knowledge areas for this area of expertise (AOE). Requirements include knowing what knowledge management is, including the history and background; and an appreciation of the range of activities and initiatives used to establish an environment where knowledge is created, shared, and used to increase competitive advantage and customer satisfaction.

The practitioner should know how technology supports the knowledge-sharing process, including information architecture, database management, and systems analysis and design. Also required is an understanding of primary business processes, including experience with the organization's operations, business tools, and business process analysis; strategies and approaches for managing culture change; adult learning theory, and After Action Review (AAR) methodology. These key knowledge areas were used to make up the chapters of the *Managing Organizational Knowledge* module.

Three of these chapters link to other modules of the *ASTD Learning System*. Chapter 4, "Understanding Business Processes" refers to Chapter 13 of Module 6, "Business Models, Drivers, and Competitive Position." Chapter 10, "Strategies to Manage Culture Change," refers to Chapter 5 of Module 5, "Organizational Systems, Culture, and Political Dynamics." Chapter 11, "Adult Learning Theory," refers to Chapter 1 of Module 1, "Cognition and Adult Learning Theory." These crossover chapters contain key knowledge relating to this particular AOE, and can be found in detail elsewhere in the *ASTD Learning System*.

Closely related to key knowledge are key actions. These include the behaviors and activities required for an individual to perform effectively in the AOE. Usually, key actions are easily observable and portray the daily work of WLP professionals. Following the key actions are outputs, or what the professional delivers. Some examples of key actions and their related outputs for Managing Organizational Knowledge are listed in the following table.

Key Actions (Do)	Examples of Outputs (Deliver)
• Design and implement knowledge management (KM) solutions • Create a KM infrastructure	• Systems providing access to information • Analysis, summaries, and reports of knowledge • Knowledge map
• Leverage technology • Manage information life cycle	• Records of knowledge management use (such as frequency of system access)
• Encourage collaboration • Establish a knowledge culture • Transform knowledge into learning • Champion knowledge management	• Strategy/plan for knowledge sharing within the organization
• Benchmark KM best practices and lessons learned • Evaluate KM success	• After Action Review document • Evaluation data

For further detailed information about the key knowledge, key actions, and outputs, refer to the *ASTD Competency Study: Mapping the Future* (2004).*

*Bernthal, P.R., et al. (2004). *ASTD Competency Study: Mapping the Future*. Alexandria, VA: ASTD Press.

1
Concepts, Philosophy, and Theory

Knowledge management (KM) is the combination of organizational culture, strategic goals, individual needs, and the expertise of its people to create an atmosphere of learning and growth. Philosophically, knowledge management must be a vital part of corporate principles and individual jobs for knowledge sharing to succeed. It's through its conceptual components that knowledge management becomes legitimate.

Assessing and meeting each person's needs is essential to the process. Through the use of this knowledge, people and organizations can improve. As people improve, so do an organization's strategic goals.

Learning Objectives:

☑ Express the concepts of knowledge management.

☑ List the components of knowledge management.

☑ Define the goals of knowledge management.

Information Versus Instruction

Information management is key in every organization. There are two primary traditions of providing essential information: instruction and sharing. ***Instruction*** is information that's taught. When a learning need requires instruction, training is provided. Instruction may include information incorporating corporate ideals, expectations, safety, and related materials and can be delivered via classroom instruction, e-learning, and on-the-job training.

Information sharing can be done informally or formally. When a learning need is more appropriately addressed with information, knowledge management may be the solution. Information sharing and knowledge management occur in organizations that encourage sharing information and use collaboration, mentoring, and socialization to inform people. This information sharing can be done at the workstation, in meetings, or as issues happen.

As Rosenberg (2001) points out, providing access to information enables employees to access the organization's collective wisdom. Although both instruction and information aid learning, they are different in many respects, as shown in Table 1-1.

Knowledge Management Concepts

Knowledge and information are increasingly becoming key assets for organizations. Three key terms to understand as the building blocks for knowledge management include data, information, and knowledge, as Groff and Jones (2003) explain:

- ***Data:*** The nature of data is raw and without context and can exist in any form, usable or not. For example, numbers in a spreadsheet are data.

- ***Information:*** Data that has been given meaning. Spreadsheets are often used to create information from a set of data, such as sales over a period of time, increases or decreases in sales, competitor trends, and so on.

- ***Knowledge:*** Information that when combined with understanding enables action. For example, a manager analyzing a declining sales trend may take action to identify issues and carry out strategies to change the trend.

Think of the relationship of data, information, and knowledge as a hierarchy. Data gets turned into information, which then provides knowledge on which decisions are based. The key for organizations to harness the power of knowledge management is to turn information into accessible and reusable knowledge.

There are two main types of knowledge:

- ***Tacit:*** This type of knowledge refers to personal knowledge in one's head—knowing how to do something based on experience. It includes judgment, insights, experience, know-how as well as personal beliefs and values. For example, when conducting web-based training for the first time, a trainer can read documented information about how to conduct this training but at this point lacks tacit knowledge—the know-how based on previous experience.

Table 1-1. Comparing Training, Knowledge Management, and Performance Support

	Training	Knowledge Management	Performance Support
Purpose	To instruct	To inform	To guide performance directly
Interruption of work	Requires interruption to participate	Requires less interruption than training	Less interruption from work (should aim to be integrated with work tasks)
How users learn	Program defines content and instruction	User defined	Task at hand defines what the tool does
Goal	Transfer knowledge or skill	To be a resource for users	To assist performance or completion of a task

- **Explicit:** This type of knowledge includes information that has been documented or can be shared with someone. For example, a trainer may not have conducted web-based training before, but based on what the trainer has read and heard from others, he or she may know the exact sequencing of steps to log in to the Web session and conduct the training.

So what exactly is knowledge management? ***Knowledge management*** is the explicit and systematic management of intellectual capital and organizational knowledge as well as the associated processes of creating, gathering, organizing, retrieving, leveraging, and using intellectual capital for the purposes of improving organizations and the people in them.

Through these processes, organizations capture and store data and information in a central or distributed electronic environment—often referred to as a ***knowledge base***. Many organizations are using knowledge bases to turn tacit knowledge (individual know-how) into explicit knowledge (documented information, steps, and processes). As noted by Groff and Jones, turning tacit knowledge into explicit knowledge is one of the key functions of a knowledge management strategy.

Knowledge Management Elements

So how do organizations transform their current structure and processes to become learning organizations that leverage knowledge management? Marquardt (1996) provides some insight into these knowledge management elements:

- *Collaboration and the ability to connect individuals or groups:* Everyone in organizations should be encouraged to gather data through the Internet, various media, internal data management systems, and socialization with peers and co-workers and to share this information across the organization. For example, some organizations may hold rallies in which teams and individual employees are encouraged to share ideas as well as strategic reviews, system audits, internal benchmarking reports, and symposiums that bring together customers, suppliers, internal groups, and external experts to share ideas and learn from one another.

- *Nature of expertise and access to experts:* Many organizations encourage team mixing and job rotations to facilitate transferring knowledge across boundaries by having people or teams possessing knowledge work with other groups or departments. This approach facilitates sharing new approaches and perceptions that new people bring to a situation. As Marquardt points out, "He or she is more likely to raise the 'dumb questions' that lead to new insight about how to handle a problem."

- *Communities of practice enable employees to access specific groups to post issues, solve problems, or discuss key topics:* A **community of practice** generally means a group of people who share a common interest in an area of competence and are willing to share the experiences of their practice. Many organizations encourage people to gather data that might benefit the organization. One channel for gaining this knowledge is communities of practice, which may be groups that meet formally, web boards where questions and answers are posted, and other types of collaboration tools, such as message and chat boards. For example, a group of scientists on a LAN may collaborate, share notes, and raise questions.

- *Knowledge networking connects groups of people with systems and applications:* For knowledge management to work, data and information must be captured in a system or central repository. This information must be coded a certain way so that it makes sense to employees trying to search for and access it. Organizations must decide the value of data and the system used to codify this information. The stored knowledge should be readily accessible to everyone in the organization and made available in a logical manner—for example, by topical categories and key words.

- *Making real-time information available to people who need it, when they need it:* The key concept in knowledge management is providing information to the right people, in the right format, and in the right period of time. Many decisions have a time element attached to them, and information that's not readily available to provide insight may mean a missed opportunity to make the right decision. Systems must be readily accessible for employees to search for and access key information when it's needed.

- *Knowledge of organization depth and scope:* Many organizations collect volumes of data, but unless it's coded and stored in a way that makes sense to employees and is retrievable, it's just volumes of data. Organizations need to determine what data to capture, how to capture it, and the format for providing information for employees to analyze it and make decisions.

- *Personalization and navigation of the system and interface:* In many organizations, employees aren't computer savvy. As a result, they may not be fully aware of the importance of retaining this data and entering it into a centralized system. For employees trying to retrieve data from a knowledge management system, ease of use and ability to quickly access the exact information they need enhances employees' compliance to enter and access data from a centralized system.

- *A key difference between information and instruction:* Information is data that has been given meaning. Organizations that encourage sharing information use collaboration, mentoring, and socialization to inform people. This can be done at workstations, in meetings, or as issues happen. Instruction is information that's taught, for example, in on-the-job training or in classroom and web instruction.

Knowledge Management Goals

An abundance of information is available on the Internet, some of it well organized and some of it not. The goal of knowledge management is the effective sharing of knowledge throughout an organization for the benefit of the organization or the individual. This includes orientation information to fit culture and skills specific to socialization knowledge. This information needs to prepare an individual for success and prepare the organization for successful outcomes. Knowledge management seeks to overcome the barriers in knowledge sharing, such as collaboration.

As Rosenberg points out, "Many KM systems are facilitated by Internet technologies. Yet despite the need for technology, knowledge management is as much about people, working relationships, and communication. Live teamwork, collaboration, and other forms of person-to-person interaction are essential to create the right balance between the information and the actions of people."

✓ **Chapter 1 Knowledge Check**

1. **Knowledge management is the explicit and systematic management of intellectual capital and is concerned with turning explicit knowledge into tacit knowledge.**

   __ **A.** True

   __ **B.** False

2. **Which type of knowledge refers to personal knowledge in one's head, or knowing how to do something based on experience? It includes judgment, insights, experience, know-how, personal beliefs, and values.**

   __ **A.** Explicit

   __ **B.** Tacit

   __ **C.** Psychomotor

   __ **D.** Cognitive

3. **A WLP professional is conducting a study on the effects of a training program she is delivering. She is drawing on her own experiences to guide the study. What type of knowledge is being represented by the professional?**

   __ **A.** Data

   __ **B.** Tacit

   __ **C.** Information

   __ **D.** Explicit

4. **All the following are elements of knowledge management *except***

   __ **A.** Classroom instruction

   __ **B.** Collaboration

   __ **C.** Access to subject matter experts

   __ **D.** Communities of practice

5. **Which best describes a central or distributed environment in which an organization captures and stores data?**

   __ **A.** Database management system

   __ **B.** Knowledge networking

   __ **C.** Community of practice

   __ **D.** Knowledge base

6. **Instruction is information that is shared formally or informally.**

  ___ **A.** True

  ___ **B.** False

7. **Which type of knowledge includes information that has been documented or can be shared with someone else?**

  ___ **A.** Explicit

  ___ **B.** Tacit

  ___ **C.** Psychomotor

  ___ **D.** Cognitive

8. **Which of the following best describes the key goal of knowledge management?**

  ___ **A.** To understand how employees learn best on the job and to share this information with others

  ___ **B.** To effectively share knowledge throughout an organization for the benefit of the organization or the individual

  ___ **C.** To identify performance gaps and the appropriate solutions to close gaps and to use information sharing to close those gaps

  ___ **D.** To make training program information more accessible on the job and enhance the sharing of knowledge and information

9. **A trainer is working with a team of specialists who require a collaborative information-sharing environment to help them stay up to date on the latest technology advancements. Based on this information, what can be said about this group and knowledge management?**

  ___ **A.** The collaborative requirements align with the goals of knowledge management

  ___ **B.** The highly technical nature of this group does not fit the goals of knowledge management

  ___ **C.** The group cannot get up to date on the technologies quickly enough using knowledge management

  ___ **D.** The goals of knowledge management are limited to the value the Internet can provide

10. **In building an effective knowledge management system, a training manager begins to construct a web management tool to allow employees to access vital and timely information from anywhere. He then takes prerecorded messages from the president of the company and places the clips on the site for employees to also view at their leisure. Next, he looks to extend the balance of the offering by**

__ **A.** Providing access to the company store for supplies

__ **B.** Developing a location to track client complaints around service

__ **C.** Creating a collaboration area for people to meet and discuss ideas with others in the company

__ **D.** Developing an electronic signature tool to make virtual authorizations possible

References

Groff, T.R., and T.P. Jones. (2003). *Introduction to Knowledge Management.* Burlington, MA: Butterworth-Heinemann.

Marquardt, M. (1996). *Building the Learning Organization.* New York: McGraw-Hill.

Newman, A. (1999). "Knowledge Management." *Infoline* No. 259903.

Nonaka, I., and H. Takeuchi. (1995). *The Knowledge-Creating Company.* New York: Oxford University Press.

Rosenberg, M.J. (2001). *E-Learning: Strategies for Delivering Knowledge in the Digital Age.* New York: McGraw-Hill.

Rumizen, M. (2002). *The Complete Idiot's Guide to Knowledge Management.* Madison, WI: CWL Publishing.

Voosen, D., and P. Conneely. (2002). "Building Learning Communities." *Infoline* No. 250208.

2
History and Best Practices

The history of knowledge management begins with the recognition that tapping into an organization's knowledge is essential for efficiency, effectiveness, and satisfaction of customers and employees. Factors that have influenced the appreciation of knowledge in organizations include programs that offer structured education and sharing, the creation of human resources development (HRD) departments, the identification of the effectiveness of informal and incidental learning, the Internet, and the explanation and availability of electronic performance support systems (EPSSs). The role of learning and sharing in the past was limited and fractioned. Only those who needed information received it.

Fiscal concerns prompted the need for skills explanation, shared roles, expanding responsibilities, and making effective use of staff. Knowledge mapping, an important aspect of knowledge management, recognizes that information is flexible. The explosion of knowledge management is a result of the electronic opportunities available to organizations. Information, education, and networking become fingertip actions. The Internet and electronic learning programs are the most important causes of the development of a knowledge highway, from a vision in the future to present-day reality.

Learning Objectives:

- ☑ Summarize the history and roots of knowledge management.
- ☑ Define best practice processes with regard to knowledge management and list several examples.

History of Knowledge Management

Many theorists have contributed to the evolution of knowledge management, among them Peter Drucker, Karl-Erik Sveiby, and Peter Senge. Models and frameworks help workplace learning and performance (WLP) professionals think of information in a new way and communicate ideas and concepts to peers. Many theorists discuss knowledge management from two perspectives:

- *Knowledge can be viewed as an object:* Many types of learning content management systems use the term "knowledge objects" to define the pieces of content that may be used to build a course.

- *Knowledge can be viewed as a process:* Knowledge can be used to assess, change, and improve human skills and behavior. Ultimately, the focus is to make knowledge available when it's needed to change human behavior.

Some theorists believe that knowledge management began in the 1950s when Alfred Sloan was at General Motors. By 1990, a number of consulting firms had started in-house knowledge management programs, and several well-known U.S., European, and Japanese firms instituted knowledge management as well as knowledge mapping and brainstorming techniques.

Based on Peter Drucker's work, Sloan theorized that workforces became less industrialized and workers became more knowledge based as the twentieth century approached. According to Rumizen (2002), "Knowledge workers are minds, not hands. They are educated and have experience. They are hired for what they know—at work they need information and knowledge as they apply theoretical and analytical knowledge. They see work as a source of satisfaction, a place to create and produce. They must continuously learn and they'll probably have several careers over the course of their lives."

The total quality management (TQM) focus and initiatives of analyzing business processes for continuous improvement also paved the way for knowledge management. In an effort to continually improve processes, capture lessons learned, and document best practices, all this information needed to be documented, captured in repositories, and then retrieved as needed.

In the 1990s, knowledge management initiatives grew in large part because of the Internet. The International Knowledge Management Network (IKMN) began in Europe in 1989 and went online in 1994. The U.S.-based Knowledge Management Forum and other KM-related groups and publications soon joined it. Electronic performance support systems (EPSS) enabled organizations to begin capturing internal documents, best practices, and information to support on-the-job knowledge needs. As knowledge management continued to evolve, several other factors continued to contribute to this discipline, including

- research in informal and incidental learning

- structured on-the-job learning

- individual development planning and knowledge transfer

- institutional culture and organizational development research and theories

- focus and research on expert systems.

Best Practices

Best practices are techniques that are believed to constitute a paradigm of excellence in a particular field (Groff and Jones 2003). A key focus of knowledge management includes processes to create, capture, organize, share, and leverage knowledge, but best practices focus on the leveraging aspect. As Groff and Jones point out, "KM seeks to establish forums where best practices can be shared, defined, refined, debunked, or disseminated. Best practices can only be best if they are continually reviewed and revitalized because today's best practice can often become tomorrow's worst nightmare."

The point of best practices is to take a rational approach and discover proven information instead of using an intuitive approach. As Marquardt (1996) points out, searching for best practices helps an organization look externally and examine organizations with different cultures and habits. For this reason, benchmarking best practices helps organizations manage change and performance improvement. Best practices often establish benchmarks that organizations can use in measuring improvement. Benchmarking may be process oriented, performance oriented, or strategically oriented.

According to Ralph E. Grubb, the instructional systems development model that we know today is the result of a best practice process. Former U.S. President Lyndon Johnson created the Great Society program during his administration. One such program focused on inner-city youth and this population's high unemployment rate and sought to provide training to this group—hence, the U.S. Job Corps was created. The U.S. Job Corps attempted to marry training practices in big business with targeted programs for inner-city youth. The program went on for years, and as the Johnson administration came to a close, an effort to collect the best practices of what had been learned from working with unemployed inner-city youth ensued. Robert K. Branson at Florida State University led the initiative to collect these best practices for the Training and Doctrine Command of the U.S. military. The original instructional systems development (ISD) model as it's known today is the result of best practices and lessons learned that was collated into a systematic model.

It's through best practices, sometimes referred to as "best of breed," that organizations can use the history of knowledge to benefit its customers and employees. Best practices include the processes of developing, sharing, preserving, and improving expertise. Organizations use several techniques to capture and share best practices:

- *Collaboration:* Involves two or more people, departments, and companies working together for the success of the organization's people, processes, and future livelihood. It focuses on dialogue and interacting with others to learn more, generate ideas, and share knowledge.

- *Information chunking:* Seeks to reduce information into codified, categorized, reusable content. Information chunking enables organizations to create short reference materials containing relevant information. This type of information is often seen in technical reports as text boxes or table information. Information chunking should be logical and convenient information documented in an easy-to-use format. By creating these snippets, information is shared quickly and with clarity.

- *Readability:* Knowledge is difficult to share and leverage when the content isn't documented clearly. Knowledge management requires capturing and organizing documentation in a logical way to convey understanding. Organizations also need to take into account the effect language differences may have on employees' ability to understand information.

- *Personification:* Emphasizes how people see things based on what type of information they were given. For example, when looking at best-of-breed information for excellent customer service between Lands' End and Dell, WLP professionals need to recognize that the services these two customer service organizations provide are dissimilar. For that reason, Lands' End may look at the best practices Dell's customer service organization is using and apply it through a filter that could work with Lands Ends' environment, systems, and processes.

- *Pursuit and exploit:* Knowledge management seeks to make information readily available when it's needed. However, if employees don't access or leverage the information, the process stops. Organizations need to encourage, and perhaps even reward, employees for actively seeking out new information and applying the key concepts and ideas that result from sharing this information.

- *Measurement for performance improvement:* Measurement is critical to best practices because elements for improvement are identified through collecting and analyzing data. The focus of total quality management is continuous improvement. Several evaluation models and techniques may be used to measure improvement, including benchmarking and evaluation methods.

In best practices, the goal is continuous improvement. Combining historical perspective and best practices promotes workplace learning in organizations. These tools and elements help WLP professionals prepare goals and plans for effective education. The plan for improving organizational knowledge uses formal (classroom, lecture), informal (on-the-job training, shadowing, mentoring, interacting with co-workers), and nonformal (socialized, practical application) learning to benefit the strategic process.

✓ **Chapter 2 Knowledge Check**

1. **All of the following contributed to the history of knowledge management *except***

   __ **A.** On-the-job learning

   __ **B.** Structured compensation systems

   __ **C.** The access and technology of the Internet/intranets/extranets

   __ **D.** Electronic performance support systems.

2. **Knowledge can be viewed as an object and as a process.**

   __ **A.** True

   __ **B.** False

3. **A trainer is learning about the origin of knowledge management. Which of the following statements is *not* a fact about the beginnings of the concept?**

   __ **A.** It is believed to have been started at General Motors back in the 1950s

   __ **B.** It is thought to have gained its popularity as a tool for total quality management (TQM)

   __ **C.** Peter Drucker is considered to be "the father of knowledge management" because of his work in the area

   __ **D.** EPSS was an additional boost to knowledge management

4. **Collaboration involves two or more people, departments, and companies working together for the success of the organization's people, processes, and future livelihood.**

   __ **A.** True

   __ **B.** False

5. **Which of the following is *not* an example of best practices for knowledge management in an organization?**

   __ **A.** Information chunking

   __ **B.** Measurement

   __ **C.** Explicit knowledge

   __ **D.** Collaboration

6. **Which of the following best describes how measurement is used to improve best practices?**

___ **A.** The goal of best practices is continuous improvement, and without measurement, there's no benchmark to know whether processes and metrics are improving.

___ **B.** The goal of best practices is to boost employee morale. Level 1 evaluation helps determine employee reaction and change in attitude.

___ **C.** The goal of best practices is to facilitate cultural change. Through analysis and measurement, organizations can plan for and measure the effect of change on employees and the organization.

___ **D.** The goal of best practices is to identify and close performance gaps. Without measurement, the nature of the gap is unknown, and the appropriate intervention can't be selected.

7. **A trainer is looking at several knowledge management best practices. Which of the following is *not* considered a best practice in knowledge management?**

___ **A.** Collaboration

___ **B.** Personification

___ **C.** Readability

___ **D.** Managing

8. **A WLP professional is creating short reference materials containing codified, categorized, reusable content to enable people to quickly find and easily understand the information. What best practice does this activity refer to?**

___ **A.** Pursuit and exploit

___ **B.** Readability

___ **C.** Information chunking

___ **D.** Measurement

References

Barclay, R.O., and P.C. Murray. (1997). "What is Knowledge Management?" *Knowledge Praxis.* Knowledge Management Associates. Available at http://www.media-access.com /whatis.html.

Clark, D. (1999). "A Time Capsule of Learning and Training." Available at http:// www. nwlink.com/~donclark/hrd/history/knowledge.html.

Groff, T.R., and T.P. Jones. (2003). *Introduction to Knowledge Management.* Burlington, MA: Butterworth-Heinemann.

Marquardt, M. (1996). *Building the Learning Organization.* New York: McGraw-Hill.

Newman, A. (1999). "Knowledge Management." *Infoline* No. 259903.

Rumizen, M. (2002). *The Complete Idiot's Guide to Knowledge Management.* Madison, WI: CWL Publishing.

Wiig, K.M. (1997). "Knowledge Management: Where Did It Come from, and Where Will It Go?" *Journal of Expert Systems with Applications.* pp. 1-14.

3
Activities and Initiatives

Knowledge mapping is a process that connects information, education, expertise, and practical application of people in the organization for the purposes of sharing and access. It uses all methods of information sharing: formal, informal, and nonformal. A systematic plan must be developed to identify owners of information, identify those who could use the information, and identify a way to provide information in a timely and seamless manner. An organization that values knowledge mapping communicates better, solves problems better, and responds effectively to a changing environment. However, knowledge mapping isn't possible if the organizational leadership is not open; leadership must be willing to share information.

Knowledge mapping is personal. It identifies the organization's experts, best communicators, and best practices in an effort to clarify the roads to information in an organization. Any member of the organization should be able to follow this identified map for information. During the knowledge mapping process, an organization must ensure that individuals are not left out of the map—or knowledge sharing will be hindered.

An open, positive attitude by organizational leaders is essential for knowledge sharing, which is the goal of knowledge mapping. If organizational leadership is not open, supportive, or innovative, then knowledge mapping and knowledge management will not succeed. When pathways for information are clearly defined, then individuals can seek needed information without fear or barriers.

Learning Objectives:

☑ Define the purpose and process of knowledge mapping in an organization.

☑ List the key principles of knowledge mapping.

☑ Describe the importance of understanding the corporate culture and leadership prior to implementing a knowledge management initiative.

☑ List an example where management's attitude can hinder knowledge management in an organization.

☑ List three examples and considerations of how reward and incentive systems can support a knowledge management initiative.

☑ Define two means of capturing knowledge in an organization.

☑ Describe the process for establishing knowledge management support in an organization.

☑ List five effects of knowledge management within an organization.

Knowledge Mapping in an Organization

So how do organizations give employees a roadmap for finding information that resides in the minds of other employees? The primary purpose for creating a knowledge map is to point employees to where to find expertise when they need it. Rather than rely on employees to track down information, organizations may create knowledge maps to identify sources of information that would otherwise be difficult to find.

According to Davenport and Prusak (1998), "a knowledge map—whether it is an actual map, a knowledge 'Yellow Pages,' or a cleverly constructed database—points to knowledge but does not contain it. It is a guide, not a repository. Developing a knowledge map involves locating important information in the organization and then publishing some sort of list or picture that shows where to find it. Knowledge maps typically point to people as well as to documents and databases."

Purpose of Knowledge Mapping

Knowledge mapping often involves

- taking an inventory of what people in the organization have documented

- surveying what information has been entered into information systems

- identifying sources of information employees use that come from external resources, such as websites.

Davenport and Prusak point out that just as a city map shows resources (libraries, hospitals, and school) and how to get to them, a knowledge map is a picture of what exists in an organization and how to get there. Knowledge mapping should make it possible to

- Discover the location, ownership, value, and use of knowledge

- Learn the roles and expertise of people

- Identify constraints to the flow of knowledge

- Spot opportunities to leverage existing knowledge.

As noted by Davenport and Prusak, using an organizational chart is a poor substitute for a knowledge map. Organizational charts may show employees where to look based on a job title; however, they don't indicate exactly where people should find knowledge. In most cases, employees have to cross functional boundaries to find information.

Knowledge-Mapping Process

When compiling a knowledge map, most of the knowledge already exists with employees in the organization. The challenge is in gathering and organizing information. Organizations often use surveys or knowledge audits to synthesize data. **Knowledge surveys** collect the type of information employees have as well as the type of information they need to do their jobs. **Knowledge audits** clarify the type of information employees need and highlight any barriers to sharing organizational knowledge. They identify repositories of information and their location, and then focus on knowledge processes and workflow.

During this process, map makers may identify more information based on a **snowball sample**—meaning that when one employee mentions resources and people who have knowledge, researchers talk with those employees, find more resource names and information, and so on.

Key Principles of Knowledge Mapping

According to Karl Wiig (2004), "Knowledge mapping covers several approaches to obtain an overview of the state of knowledge assets and knowledge flow within an area, the full enterprise, or within a region or country. Knowledge mapping may be part of, or combined with, other approaches such as knowledge surveys. Typical knowledge maps, in addition to providing descriptions of the knowledge assets and flows, will also provide pictorial maps that may indicate locations of assets, flows of knowledge, relationships between workflows and knowledge assets, and other significant aspects such as the quality of vulnerability of knowledge situations in different . . . business functions."

Some key principles of knowledge mapping include

- Knowledge is transient.

- To build trust and facilitate sharing information in an organization, explain the goal of this process and establish boundaries, including respecting personal disclosures from employees.

- A number of forms of knowledge need to be identified and gathered. Some types of knowledge include tacit and explicit, formal and informal, codified and personalized, internal and external, and short life cycle or permanent.

- Knowledge resides in many locations in the organization, such as processes, relationships, policies, documents, conversations, links and context, suppliers, competitors, and customers.

- Awareness of organizational levels, cultural issues, reward systems, and timeliness of rewards is essential to ensure success of the knowledge-mapping process.

- Attention must be given to the value of information being shared, such as legal processes and protection of patents, trade secrets, and trademarks.

Corporate Culture and Leadership

Corporate culture can be a powerful force to shape an organization's overall effectiveness and long-term success.

As organizations grow, they become more specialized, expand to various geographies, the information needed by individuals to do their jobs become distributed across functional areas and geographic boundaries. Each organization is different from every other one.

The values, beliefs, behaviors, customs, and attitudes of an organization help individuals understand the organizational goals, processes, and what is considered important.

When trying to understand corporate culture, WLP professionals need to determine the overall feel of the organization by understanding the day-to-day roles of individuals and the business context.

Formal change management initiatives transform organizations from the current state to the desired state through a series of carefully planning initiatives and actions. As noted by Rumizen (2002), "By changing the way people behave, by showing them that new ways of working make them more successful, and by creating a new and shared history, you affect the underlying assumptions that drive behavior in the first place."

Attitude of Management

Several challenges can potentially hinder using a knowledge management process, including the attitude of management. For example, management may have a negative assumption that employees on a knowledge portal are surfing and not doing their jobs—when in fact they could be searching for or collaborating with others to gain knowledge for solving a problem.

For knowledge management to take hold and grow in an organization, management must give people time to search for information as required and when needed to facilitate organizational knowledge, processes, and growth. Marquardt (1996) notes that in learning organizations, everyone should be encouraged to gather data and to understand how this process might provide value to the organization. An effective way to transfer knowledge is to transfer individuals or teams who possess the knowledge—and they in turn can ensure that the knowledge has been transferred.

Rewards and Incentives

Organizations have to change to survive, and appropriate rewards and incentives can help employees and management embrace change and use knowledge management systems and processes. In smaller organizations, rewards can be linked directly to organizational success by sharing and leveraging knowledge and lessons learned.

In larger organizations, rewarding employee performance as it relates to knowledge management may be most beneficial. For example, rewarding employees for sharing specific knowledge, facilitating knowledge management processes, documenting best practices, and being compliant in using other support tools helps develop faster and more efficient problem solving. Linking knowledge management and processes into organizational goals, departmental goals, and down to individual goals helps align employee behavior and drive desired performance—especially if rewards and incentives support this behavior.

Organizations need to develop an environment and culture that encourages everyone to share knowledge through incentives as well. Many employees think their job security is based in part on the knowledge or skills they have, which may be in limited quantity in the organization. By sharing knowledge, an organization can build more experts in specific areas. Incentives and rewards help drive the desired behavior—including sharing knowledge—if conveyed and positioned correctly.

Capturing Knowledge

Several techniques can be leveraged as a means of capturing knowledge:

- Record all brainstorming sessions. In brainstorming, a group provides a list of ideas before any ideas are evaluated for their merit and viability to carry out. Although some brainstormed ideas may not be used at that point in time, by compiling and maintaining a list of all ideas, the organization is capturing a list of possible solutions that might work for solving future situations.

- Establish formal problem-solving processes and guidelines for documenting discussions and outputs. By setting up formal processes and procedures, networked employees can post questions or issues to an organization's intranet problem-solving area. This area is also monitored by employees who then respond to postings with possible solutions they have tried with successful results.

- Another technique involves a gathering session for employees to leverage information from multiple disciplines or cross-functional areas. These gathering sessions help employees throughout the organization meet in disparate groups. The groups are given problems or issues to solve—giving ownership for problems to the people who do the work and perform the processes every day.

Knowledge Management Support

Now that some key components for the success of knowledge management in an organization have been outlined, it's important to see what support factors must be in place to begin a knowledge management initiative in an organization that's set up for success.

1. Begin with targeted projects specific to the organization.

2. Tie the project directly to discrete business requirements and opportunities.

3. Keep the language simple and focused.

4. Be careful of the technology used.

5. Start small by using pilot programs first rather than departments trying to carry out knowledge management.

6. Involve the people who will use the information, systems, tools, and processes from the start of the process.

7. Scrutinize what can and can't be included as knowledge material.

Effects of Knowledge Management

Organizations instituting knowledge management in their environments often see a series of effects from this initiative. Some benefits are discussed in the following sections.

Introduction of Metrics

Setting target metrics and benchmarking measures is a way to link task output to organizational goals. For organizations to be successful, they need to identify critical success measures and evaluate performance through return-on-investment (ROI) or other evaluation methods. Knowledge management is a strategic initiative leading to a competitive advantage. Because of this strategic nature, it will have staying power and ongoing viability.

Implementation of Metrics

Process reviews and lessons learned are gathered and added to a knowledge repository to be accessed for future use. Statistical information can be used to gauge use of the knowledge management system and accumulate the number of employees accessing and attending online collaborations. Increased internal use of search engines to access information and sharing of information via email messages, web boards, and other collaboration tools helps to support the value of knowledge management in an organization.

Improved Quality of Information

The quality of information in an organization improves organizational quality and is more timely because of the focus on knowledge management and becoming a learning organization. Employees have the ability to provide feedback, and with this feedback, knowledge sharing, and workflow audit trailing, improvements for raw material quality and quantity are identified. With high-quality information, the need for editing and rework decreases, too. Employees gain quicker access to information on Internet or intranet sites via links (known as "favorites") created to the information.

Information Updates

Increased focus on updating information ensures that the most current information is available when needed. Some organizations gauge the average age of content pages on an intranet site and then evaluate the number of pages older than a specific age and the number of pages past their review date. This type of analysis helps ensure that lists of potentially outdated pages are reviewed. This type of analysis can be broken down by content owner or business group.

Maintenance Updates

Reduced maintenance costs are often another benefit of knowledge management because employees have direct data access, so library staff are no longer needed. As a result, employees become more efficient and self-sufficient in being able to locate and access information when and where they need it. Employees also reduce the time needed to complete tasks and solve problems with the readily available and easy-to-retrieve nature of information. Organizations also see a reduction in expenses in terms of printing and transaction costs.

Improved Customer Metrics

Because of the ability to access information and provide answers quickly, customer service metrics may improve. This improvement may lead to increased sales, better customer relationship management, quicker response to leads, increased customer satisfaction, and more repeat orders. As a result, customers experience more consistency in information and advice from the organization.

Increase in Staff Morale

As a result of knowledge management, employee morale may increase because of the ability to access information quickly and give responses more readily to internal and external clients. Organizations can quickly gather employee feedback on morale and assess and devise better policies and processes.

✓ Chapter 3 Knowledge Check

1. **Which of the following best describes knowledge mapping?**

    __ **A.** A process involving two or more people, departments, and companies working together for the success of the organization's people, processes, and future livelihood

    __ **B.** A process of capturing, organizing, and storing information and experiences of workers and groups in an organization and making them available to others

    __ **C.** A process that identifies the location, ownership, value, and use of information and knowledge.

    __ **D.** A process that identifies and closes performance gaps. Without measurement, the nature of the gap is unknown, and the appropriate solution can't be selected

2. **Some types of knowledge include tacit and explicit, formal and informal, and short and imperative.**

    __ **A.** True

    __ **B.** False

3. **A training manager is trying to conduct a knowledge survey to determine the origin of a vital training exercise. As she works with one of the founding partners, she discovers some information that refers her to several persons and other documents detailing vital pieces of information that make up this knowledge base. Based on the information above, this is an example of snowball sampling.**

    __ **A.** True

    __ **B.** False

4. **Corporate culture does not have an effect on knowledge management in an organization.**

    __ **A.** True

    __ **B.** False

5. **The attitude of management can help or hinder knowledge management in an organization.**

    __ **A.** True

    __ **B.** False

6. **A training manager is constructing an incentive plan for encouraging behavioral change. The behaviors being targeted link directly to a new collaborative tool that is being promoted internally to help facilitate virtual meetings. This description is an example of implementing an incentive program in support of knowledge management.**

   __ **A.** True

   __ **B.** False

7. **The following are all examples of ways to capture knowledge in an organization *except***

   __ **A.** Recording brainstorming sessions

   __ **B.** Establishing formal problem-solving guidelines and processes

   __ **C.** Conducting performance reviews

   __ **D.** Holding a gathering session for team members from cross-functional groups

8. **The following are all examples of ways to establish support for knowledge management in an organization *except***

   __ **A.** Tying the project to business requirements and opportunities

   __ **B.** Scrutinizing what can and cannot be included as knowledge material

   __ **C.** Selecting the most advanced technology available

   __ **D.** Beginning with targeted projects

9. **Organizations often see an improvement in the introduction and implementation of metrics after instituting knowledge management.**

   __ **A.** True

   __ **B.** False

References

Davenport, T.H., and L. Prusak. (1998). *Working Knowledge.* Boston: Harvard Business School Press.

Groff, T.R., and T.P. Jones. (2003). *Introduction to Knowledge Management.* Burlington, MA: Butterworth-Heinemann.

Marquardt, M. (1996). *Building the Learning Organization.* New York: McGraw-Hill.

Newman, A. (1999). "Knowledge Management." *Infoline* No. 259903.

Rumizen, M. (2002). *The Complete Idiot's Guide to Knowledge Management.* Madison, WI: CWL Publishing.

Schein, E. (1992). *Organizational Culture and Leadership,* 2nd edition. San Francisco: Jossey-Bass.

Stevens, L. (December 2000). "Knowing What Your Company Knows." *Knowledge Management.* pp. 38–42.

Wiig, K.M. (2004). *People-Focused Knowledge Management: How Effective Decision Making Leads to Corporate Success.* Jordan Hill, Oxford: Elsevier Butterworth-Heinemann.

4
Understanding Business Processes

 To effectively develop a knowledge management system, organizations need to be able to identify and document their business processes that support knowledge exchange. By documenting these processes, an organization can streamline and automate repetitive features that expedite task completion as well as a learning process for its members. Streamlining processes entails activities such as workflow identification and management, automation of forms and queries, and the establishment of communities of practice that are supported by a knowledge exchange network.

WLP professionals need a basic understanding of how businesses function in the organization's community, how funding and revenues are determined, and what the organization's strategic strengths and weaknesses are. WLP professionals then must be able to convey learning initiatives and interventions in the terminology of their organizations so that the function is seen as a strategic business partner.

Developing and managing a strategic learning process is nearly impossible without first becoming a strategic partner in the organization. To become a strategic partner, focus on the following steps:

- Provide services that support the organization's business strategy.

- Improve the visibility of one's own activities and accomplishments.

- Measure results or at least tie results to other internal measures.

- Become educated in strategic planning.

- Educate others in the strategic-planning process.

Defining the type and state of your business correctly can lead to resounding success or embarrassing failure. In a now classic example, railroad companies defined themselves as being in the railroad business rather than the transportation business. Had they answered the question "What is your business?" correctly, they might have emerged as an exploding growth industry instead of a declining, or at best static, portion of the transportation industry. The same is true when defining the state of the industry for an organization.

Learning Objective:

☑ Discuss how documenting business processes and establishing communities of practice can support a knowledge management initiative.

Key Knowledge: Understanding Primary Processes

For the learning function to be a valued business partner, understanding the business model, business objectives, growth factors, and strategic drivers for the organization and industry is essential. In completing this analysis, WLP professionals also need to understand corporate measures of success and how success is defined and measured in the organization. All these factors drive how training programs in an organization are created and linked to the business goals and objectives.

After defining the big-picture perspective on the state of the industry, goals, and objectives, and how success is measured in the organization, WLP professionals should examine the company culture and value systems. An organization's culture—the assumptions employees share about their work and their feelings toward the organization—can't be ignored during this analysis. Assessing the culture and the degree to which it helps or hinders deployment of a strategic plan is critical to the plan's success.

Continual environmental scanning must be done to proactively assess the effect of change on an organization. A SWOT (strengths, weaknesses, opportunities, and threats) analysis, based on current and future changes in environmental trends and forces, should be performed as strengths and weaknesses shift and when the assessment uncovers new opportunities or threats.

Organizational structures help define department functions, roles and responsibilities, relationships between departments, reporting structures, organizational layout (meaning who employees exchange information with and documents and other resources used to perform their jobs), and the workflow network (the formal organizational structure supporting workflow for business processes and how each process works).

Knowledge exchanges, also known as knowledge exchange networks, enable different groups in an organization to share documents and information on products, to create lists of links in simple webpages, and to discuss issues of mutual interest. Knowledge exchanges can benefit the organization in several ways. They are more flexible than traditional organizational units, cutting across geographic, sectoral, and disciplinary boundaries and formal reporting lines. They can serve as a vehicle for cultural change, creating a knowledge-sharing culture and supporting development activities, research, sharing of best practices, and other knowledge management initiatives.

For more information, see Module 6, *Managing the Learning Function,* Chapter 13, "Business Models, Drivers, and Competitive Position."

5
Business Process Analysis

Business process analysis is a structured method of documenting business rules and functions to uncover hidden inefficiencies that highlight strengths that could be streamlined or leveraged to increase productivity. This analysis attempts to standardize workflow in a manner that decreases redundancy of effort and increases information reuse. By conducting a business process analysis at an organization, requirements for effectively and efficiently capturing, storing, retrieving, and managing knowledge can be met in an organization.

Depending on the resource, definitions of what a business process includes vary from author to author as well as from organization to organization. The key to successful knowledge management is linked to logical connections to the organization's business needs. Tools and techniques should be considered as part of the analysis process and may be helpful in developing these connections.

Learning Objectives:

☑ Define the purpose of business process identification, and list several types of work processes to consider.

☑ List and describe several types of analysis tools and techniques to facilitate business process analysis.

☑ Describe the importance of project management and potential life cycle issues that WLP professionals may encounter during this process.

Business Process Identification and Discovery

Increasingly, organizations are realizing that the first step in almost any major project includes analyzing and defining business processes, and then communicating those processes to employees who need to use them. This step applies to any project, such as information technology and information management system implementations.

Total quality is a management-led effort that involves the entire organization in continuously improving work processes. This effort is customer focused and uses objective data to eliminate waste of all kinds. The goal is to achieve a breakthrough in quality to reach unprecedented levels of performance. W. Edwards Deming, the American credited with introducing statistical quality control to the Japanese in the 1950s, taught that quality improvement leads to increases in productivity and competitiveness. This in turn guarantees long-term survival for organizations.

Quality has served as a successful business strategy, and companies that are using quality principles to improve their business performance are seeing competitive advantages. The principle of quality-oriented business strategy is the focus on customer requirements. Companies focus on the business strategies of improving processes so that waste is eliminated, cycle time is reduced, and customer requirements (that is, market-perceived quality) are the focus of the entire enterprise. Organizations realize that to stay in business, they need to capitalize on the competitive advantage that total quality as well as total quality tools and techniques have to offer.

Business process analysis and design, which are the result of the total quality movement, are often prerequisites for new projects. So what is a **business process**? A process is how people, materials, methods, machines, and the environment combine to add value to a product or service. Everything that gets done is a part of the process—how the work gets done, roles and responsibilities, and resources and systems. For example, designing a training course is a process. It includes the people involved in the design, the books and articles written on the topic, how people work individually and together, the computers and copiers used, the lighting, the ventilation, and the number of distractions in the work area.

Suppliers, customers, and subprocesses are also part of the process. Suppliers include the person who hired designers and the person who ordered materials. Customers include trainers who teach the course, the participants, and their managers. A subprocess is preventive maintenance that keeps machines working properly. All these elements are part of the design process.

Variation, a part of every process, is the result of combining five elements of a process: people, machines, methods, materials, and environment. The concept of variation is important because improving processes results from reducing variation—keeping processes within well-defined control limits.

Various Workflows

A variety of problem-solving and quantitative tools and techniques is used to identify and improve business processes.. A ***process map*** is a visual tool used to systematically describe actions and behaviors in a sequential flow. A process flow or map presents a clear and logical visual representation of all the tasks and steps involved in carrying out a particular process. Unlike a simple task list, process maps are beneficial in that they graphically demonstrate decision points and their multiple selections, thus allowing branching tasks into separate paths, depending on the decision's outcome. Many organizations use various approaches toward process mapping.

Process maps are typically used to

- understand the process in order to be able to analyze and improve the process
- pinpoint problem areas and opportunities for improvement
- communicate work or process requirements
- identify the effect of work or process changes
- train staff, particularly new employees, in how to perform the work
- provide performance support to people who do not perform the process regularly.

Process mapping entails constructing a process flowchart to determine where processes begin and end. The process map can show the information needed to understand the general process flow or supply detail on every finite action and decision point. The process map shows the inputs required to start the process (such as people, machines, materials, and methods), the tasks required to perform the process, decision points, and the outputs at the end of the process.

The purpose of process mapping is to understand the current process and identify appropriate benchmarks for measuring process results. Process maps may be created to document the workflow of processes, documents, work, and e-commerce. They include a set of symbols (boxes and arrows) to indicate the basic flow of a process. Information from a process map typically includes

- process boundaries and links
- process owners
- process inputs and outputs
- process customers and suppliers.

The objectives of the project or analysis should guide the level of detail in the process map.

Process mapping must occur before process redesign can take place, an intervention designed to change the flow of activities or decisions associated with generating a specific business output. Examples of business outputs include a design for a new product, a purchase order, a product, or a service. Although business outputs may often be produced in one department, many of an organization's mission-critical processes span departmental boundaries.

Business process analysis, design, and redesign document workflow activities and decisions. Well-designed workflows tend to have the following characteristics:

- Involve groups of people who are responsible for performing the tasks.

- Use a diagramming method (such as process maps or flowcharts) to pictorially display current and future flows of activities and decisions among departments.

- Use metrics to establish performance baselines and measure progress.

- Incorporate whole-systems thinking so that process performance is aligned with other organizational variables, such as overall strategy, competitive pressures, and activities in other parts of the organization.

- Include more than small representative design groups in formulating and carrying out new processes.

- Encourage redesigners to set stretch goals (that is, goals that require considerable effort and challenge organizations to reach higher levels of performance).

Many interventions seek to redesign processes, including total quality management (TQM) and business reengineering. In addition, systems-thinking projects often result in changes to organizational processes. Process analysis and redesign are appropriate interventions when one or more of the following root causes is attributed to the performance problem:

- Department changes of information or materials are slow, cumbersome, and inefficient.

- Decisions take longer than they should and are of low quality.

- A string of process activities that span departmental boundaries is not managed well because of turn-around issues that arise in carrying out the process.

- Bottlenecks are causing delays.

- Benchmarking data from inside or outside the organization suggests that outputs might be generated faster, more cheaply, or with higher quality.

- The spirit and culture of continuous improvement exists in the organization, and people actively seek opportunities to redesign existing workflows.

Analysis Tools and Techniques

The methodology used to identify, clarify, and improve business processes consists of a variety of problem-solving and quantitative tools and techniques most often used for diagnosing quality issues and maintaining quality control. In many organizations, time is initially spent defining the beginning and ending boundaries of preliminary business processes (where the process begins and ends). This effort enables seeing business process as a logical, manageable piece in a complex organizational task.

Several tools and techniques can be used to analyze business processes:

- Six Sigma DMAIC methodology

- Six Sigma IPO model

- flowchart diagramming

- evaluation models.

Six Sigma Processes

Six Sigma is a business-driven approach to improvement and increased customer satisfaction that Motorola originated in the mid-1980s. It's often used at an operational level to help cut costs, reduce errors or defects, improve processes, and reduce business cycle times. In the mid-1990s, Motorola shared the details of this framework—which has since been leveraged by other large manufacturing organizations. This framework is a data-driven approach to analyzing and solving root causes of business problems. It ties the outputs of a business directly to marketplace requirements. At the strategic or transformative level, the goal of Six Sigma is to align an organization to its marketplace and deliver real improvements and dollars to the bottom line. Six Sigma's primary principle seeks to improve customer satisfaction by reducing defects. The ideal performance target is defect-free process and products with 3.4 or fewer defective parts per million—or that all processes and products are 99.9997 percent defect free.

Six Sigma DMAIC Methodology

Six Sigma's focus for reduction of defects, process improvement, and customer satisfaction is guided by five key steps in the DMAIC methodology: **Define, Measure, Analyze, Improve, and Control.** Figure 5-1 shows an overview of the methodology and lists examples of some tools used in each step. These are the five steps:

- *Define:* Define the project goals and customer (internal and external) deliverables. This step includes describing the problem or opportunity in the form of a process or procedure that affects the end product's conformance to specifications.

- *Measure:* Measure the process to determine current performance and quantify the problem. This step includes defining and identifying key measurements and collecting data—most often with quality inspections using a sampling method. This step also draws a conclusion based on the collected data.

- *Analyze:* Analyze and determine the root cause(s) of the defects. This step includes examining processes, procedures, or services and identifying opportunities for improvement. At this step, data is analyzed to determine a root cause, and process maps are reviewed to identify inefficient actions.

- *Improve:* Define solutions and ideas that can be used to improve the process by eliminating defects.

- *Control:* Seek to control changes after they have been carried out by continuing to measure the process and to trace and confirm the stability of improvements as well as expected results.

The DMAIC methodology, although it looks linear in Figure 5-1, is an iterative process and includes a multitude of tools to help measure, analyze, and improve processes. Some tools and techniques in this methodology include process flowcharts, benchmarking, data collection methods, cause-and-effect (Ishikawa) diagrams, Pareto charts, five whys, brainstorming, control charts, and evaluation techniques. Later methodologies were added to the DMAIC framework to include analyzing the effect of organizational culture and experience level on processes and systems.

Six Sigma IPO Model

All organizations are composed of systems that interact with each other. The main components of any system include people, products or services, and processes. Because process thinking is the lynchpin of the Six Sigma methodology, processes are another focus. The foundation of process mapping and the ***Input/Process/Output (IPO)*** model (see Figure 5-2) is the depiction of an *input, the process or action* taken on the input, and the *outcome* or result of the action. Information for the process map often comes from direct observation of tasks or from interviews with top performers.

Figure 5-1. Six Sigma DMAIC and Examples of Tools

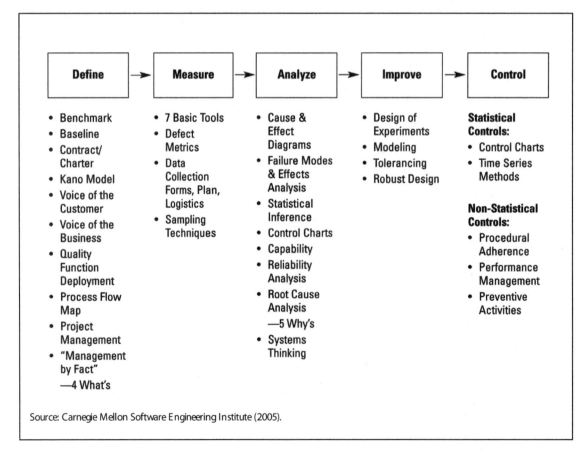

Source: Carnegie Mellon Software Engineering Institute (2005).

Figure 5-2. Six Sigma IPO Model

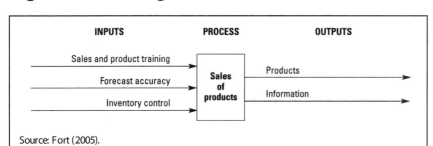

Source: Fort (2005).

Processes typically have a start and an end. Every process has inputs and outputs that can be measured, analyzed, and improved. The IPO model is a powerful tool that graphically identifies process inputs and outputs.

Flowchart Diagramming

A flowchart is a visual representation of the steps in a process and the sequence of steps. Flowcharts use standard, easily recognizable symbols connected by arrows. For example, employees at a company don't understand why it takes so long to have travel for an ASTD conference approved. A flowchart can help answer those questions by showing how many people have to sign off the expense request and how the process loops back several times through different departments.

A flowchart illustrates work or document flow for existing or proposed processes. A flowchart can also pinpoint whether the process could be simplified. It can be used to identify duplication of effort, bottlenecks, and unnecessary tasks. It can isolate problem areas and display misunderstandings. A flowchart is an excellent tool for providing a clear and orderly view of a process.

Defining process boundaries helps show what is and isn't included in a process and what the process inputs and outputs are. Flowcharts also show the departments and people involved in a particular business process. When constructing a flowchart, be sure to include the people who actually know the process best—those who actually do the work. Have the best representation of what actually occurs in real life—not what's supposed to occur according to procedures.

Flowcharting is one tool used in workflow analysis to identify both primary and secondary customers of processes. Primary customers are those who receive output from a process directly. Secondary customers receive output from a process but aren't directly needed to support the process's primary mission. With this kind of analysis, team members can clearly identify who receives output from a particular process; they understand how the work gets done, the roles and responsibilities of each person in the process, and all resources and systems used in the process.

Evaluation Models

Now that several models to define, analyze, and improve processes have been examined from a total quality perspective, evaluating whether the changes instituted have made an improvement is crucial. Many evaluation methods can be used; for example, in training WLP professionals, use Donald Kirkpatrick's Four Levels of Evaluation and Jack Phillips ROI model. Organizations need to define the appropriate level of evaluation based on their goals and objectives. Many organizations use benchmarking as a catalyst and enabler of change, a learning process rather than a scorecard. Benchmarking is used to evaluate the current quality levels of customer satisfaction or service against the best that can be identified and to work toward improving systems to exceed expected future quality levels.

Congress created the Malcolm Baldrige National Quality Award in 1987 to recognize U.S. companies that demonstrate outstanding leadership in the pursuit of quality. With the survival of many organizations hinging on higher quality of their products and services, the Malcolm Baldrige National Quality Award criteria are often a yardstick for benchmarking and evaluating the performance of organizations. For example, a past Baldrige winner, Motorola, required all its suppliers to make a serious attempt to meet the award criteria or risk losing Motorola's business. In one case, when a major airline refused to accept the Motorola challenge, an order went out from Motorola headquarters the next day for all company travel to be routed on other carriers. The airline in question changed its stance and applied the Baldrige criteria to its organization.

Applying for the Baldrige award is a tough test. For most companies, it takes the commitment of top leaders in the organization and several years to develop a quality focus for customer satisfaction. The company's processes, products, and services need to be evaluated based on customer identification and how well they fulfill customers' expectations. Stringent statistical evidence of quality levels and their improvement must be gathered and analyzed over time. Even if companies don't plan to apply for the award, however, the Baldrige award's criteria and application process have come to guide forward-looking companies in improving their operations

Project Management and Project Life Cycle Issues

Although there are many models and tools to analyze, diagnose, and improve quality issues, all these models work within a project management framework to plan and assign the work to be accomplished on time, within budget, and within scope. Project management principles are the foundation for successfully completing a project through the process of planning, organizing, and managing tasks, based on the elements of time, money, and available resources.

Project management consists of *planning, organizing,* and *controlling* work. The person responsible for project management plans for the needs of a project and then organizes and controls project resources as the project progresses. This person has one foot in the future (creating a plan), one foot in the past (learning from mistakes), and the rest of the body in the present (reacting to surprises). This role is that of the project manager.

The Project Life Cycle

The *project life cycle* is everything that happens from the beginning to the end of the project. Organizations usually divide projects into several project phases to better manage and control the project work. By managing projects in phases, project managers focus their time and energy on managing the current work but also look ahead to future phases. Collectively, the project phases are known as the project life cycle.

Typically, each phase has one or more deliverables that must be completed to end one phase and move to the next. For example, when creating a new course, the design documentation should be completed and approved before beginning the development phase. Depending on the industry and the type of work being done, the number of phases and the names of phases in the life cycle may vary.

Defining the Project and Goals

After the project manager is selected, this person and a group of people who are knowledgeable about the proposed areas (usually line managers) come together to define the project plan. Each brings to the project a unique knowledge base: execution of similar projects, personnel resources, technology availability, or quality and control. These components help the project manager define the proposed task.

The team must discuss and analyze the project and develop a firm grasp on the endeavor they're undertaking. Planning should provide answers to most of these questions:

- What are the specific goals and objectives of the project?

- How is the project going to be structured?

- What are the important tasks and events (milestones) of the project? How should they be scheduled?

- What types of personnel are needed? How will they be used?

- How are other resources (for example, money, equipment, materials, facilities) going to be distributed among various tasks?

- How will the key elements of the project—cost, performance, and schedule—be estimated and controlled? What management tools will be used?

- What are the potential bottlenecks in carrying out the project? How will they be handled?

The project-planning team should take the time to answer these questions. Project drivers and objectives should determine the project's quality and specifications and aid in assessing risk during the project.

A high degree of commitment and planning effort benefit the undertaking. To be successful, the planning team should resist the urge to forge ahead with the implementation as rapidly as possible to attain "fast track" action. Doing it right the first time requires formulating a good plan, one that's not only flexible enough to adjust to change, but also defined adequately to provide a structured method of meeting project objectives.

No matter what the specific goals are for the project's end deliverables or product, the project manager's key focus should be on scope, time, cost, quality, and resource use. If a formal project scope change is approved, the project manager needs to adjust the project scope, time (project schedule), cost, quality, and resource use, as appropriate. The project team must take the time to plan during the project's initiation stage before critical decisions are made. Any changes made later in the project result in a scope change and usually higher costs, extended time in the project schedule, or possibly lower quality specifications.

As part of the project-planning process, project teams need to prepare a risk analysis and effective contingency planning. Risk analysis can be as simple as creating a list of potential risks and identifying other strategies to eliminate the risk all together, reduce the risk, or plan for the risk and react to it if it occurs. For example, by listing and prioritizing the most likely or most negative risks that may occur, the team can develop contingencies and a list of early warning signs.

For training projects, it is during the project's planning and design phases, alpha and beta testing of programs with key stakeholders and members of the target population help provide early feedback and make it easier to carry out changes early in the process with little effect on time, cost, or quality. After the training program or intervention has been conducted, internal owners need to continually review evaluation feedback and follow up to solicit feedback from the target population. As internal processes change, any training interventions need to be updated to reflect new processes in a dynamically changing culture.

✓ Chapter 5 Knowledge Check

1. **Which of the following types of analysis attempts to standardize workflow in a manner that decreases redundancy of effort and increases information reuse?**

   __ **A.** Business process analysis

   __ **B.** System analysis

   __ **C.** System study

   __ **D.** Risk analysis

2. **A WLP professional is beginning a new major project. What should be the first step in this or any other major project?**

   __ **A.** Prepare a risk analysis

   __ **B.** Analyze and define the business processes

   __ **C.** Create a project plan for the new project

   __ **D.** Determine plans to overcome any identified project obstacles

3. **A WLP professional is constructing a process map that will be used to communicate the project to management. A process map is most typically used to**

   __ **A.** Pinpoint the problem areas and opportunities for improvement

   __ **B.** Plan, organize, and control the work involved with the project

   __ **C.** To demonstrate the proposed systematic approach in nonvisual terms

   __ **D.** To change the flow of activities or decisions associated with generating a specific business output

4. **Which of the following is a visual tool used to systematically describe actions and behaviors in a sequential flow?**

   __ **A.** DMAIC methodology

   __ **B.** Process map

   __ **C.** Evaluation models

   __ **D.** Six Sigma IPO model

5. **All of the following area examples of risk analysis and contingency planning *except***

___ **A.** A training session is scheduled to take place in Buffalo, New York., in January and all sales representatives must travel to this location. Instead, the training session location is moved to Florida.

___ **B.** A group of line workers discusses the new labor relations contract and the effect of the contract on overtime pay.

___ **C.** A group of line workers discusses inferior materials and the current scrap and rework levels. The organization decides to begin using another vendor for the raw materials.

___ **D.** A group of line workers discusses inferior materials and the effect on the manufacturing process. The department institutes a new checklist and tests to ensure that raw materials meet the minimum manufacturing standards before being put into production.

6. **Six Sigma is a business-driven approach to improvement that seeks to improve customer satisfaction by providing more effective sales and product training for the sales force.**

___ **A.** True

___ **B.** False

7. **Because all organizations are composed of systems that interact with each other, which of the following tools focuses on the main components of any system including people, products or services, and processes?**

___ **A.** Six Sigma DMAIC Methodology

___ **B.** Evaluation models

___ **C.** Flowchart diagramming

___ **D.** Six Sigma IPO model

8. **The project lifecycle is everything that happens from the beginning to the end of the project, and includes the analysis, design, development, implementation, and evaluation phases on every project.**

___ **A.** True

___ **B.** False

9. **A project manager's focus should be on**

___ **A.** Scope, time, cost, quality, and business goals

___ **B.** Scope, time, cost, quality, and product specifications

___ **C.** Scope, time, cost, quality, and resource use

___ **D.** Scope, time, cost, quality, and scope changes.

10. **A WLP professional has just constructed a 452-task project plan complete with dates and phases. Why has she chosen to incorporate phases into her project plan?**

___ **A.** To focus energy on current work with the ability to look ahead

___ **B.** All projects have phases that need to be followed

___ **C.** To demonstrate that everything is linear in the process

___ **D.** To keep people from jumping ahead of the plan

References

Beil, D., and M. Kimmel. (1991). "Fundamentals of Quality." *Infoline* No. 259111. (Out of print.)

Biech, E., and M. Danahy. (1991). "Diagnostic Tools for Total Quality." *Infoline* No. 259109. (Out of print.)

Carnegie Mellon Software Engineering Institute. (2005). "Six Sigma: Software Technology

Roadmap." Available at http://www.sei.cmu.edu/str/descriptions/sigma6_

body.html.

Fort, L. (2005). "Foundations of Six Sigma: Customer and Process." In *Six Sigma in Transactional and Service Environments*. Available at http://www.fassbex.com/articles/145.

Munro, R., and E. Rice. (1993). "The Malcolm Baldrige National Quality Award and Trainers." *Infoline* No. 259302. (Out of print.)

Renfrew, Paul. (2002). "IPO." Available at http://www.isixsigma.com/dictionary/I-P-O-491.htm.

Russell, L. (2000). *Project Management for Trainers*. Alexandria, VA: ASTD Press.

Sanders, E.S., and S. Thaigarajan. (2001). *Performance Intervention Maps*. Alexandria, VA: ASTD Press.

Six Sigma SPC's Quality Control Dictionary and Glossary. (2005). Springfield, IL: Six Sigma SPC. Available at http://www.sixsigmaspc.com/dictionary/glossary.html.

Smith, D., and J. Blakesell. (September 2002). "New Strategic Six Sigma." *T&D*. pp. 45–52.

Thompson, C. (1998) "Project Management: A Guide." *Infoline* No. 259004.

Waagen, A.K. (1998). "Task Analysis." *Infoline* No. 259808.

6
Technology and Knowledge

Technology serves as an enabler to allow organizations to capture, store, retrieve, and share institutional knowledge among its members. Developing and integrating technological tools into a business practice give an organization a powerful mechanism to support this capability. Common institutional ways in which knowledge can be shared in organizations is through content and management systems, websites, and intranet portals. Informal methods of knowledge sharing can be delivered through discussion boards, instant messaging, and chat rooms. The key to leveraging these tools successfully is to harness the ability to capture information, archive it, and retrieve it later. Only by creating the capability to capture information for future use can organizations start to build on the concept of knowledge management.

Learning Objectives:

☑ Describe the key differences between content management systems and learning content management systems.

☑ Define portals, document management systems, and collaboration tools and the role they play in supporting knowledge management in an organization.

Overview

A **knowledge repository** is a category of technology that offers products for creating, storing, and managing corporate knowledge. Ideally, users know what information is available in repositories. File systems and document management products fit into this category, as do products with a means of converting information (such as text-scanning tools).

Technology is an enabler and, therefore, can be used to help people manage knowledge. For many organizational solutions, employees must work with other departments to share and access information and content. Depending on the knowledge management system selected, organizations may need help from inside or outside the organization—to classify, codify, and organize knowledge to create a knowledge base. For organizations wanting to use technology to help employees share information, a variety of solutions are available, including

- content management systems (CMSs)

- learning content management systems (LCMSs)

- Internet and intranet portals

- document management systems

- collaboration tools.

Content Management Systems

Wikipedia defines a **content management system** (CMS) as "a computer software system for organizing and facilitating collaborative creation of documents and other content. A content management system is frequently a web application used for managing websites and web content, though in many cases, content management systems require special client software for editing and constructing articles."

Content management systems include many phases in the content lifecycle from creating content to providing it to individuals. Figure 6-1 provides an overview of this lifecycle

Figure 6-1. Content Management System Overview

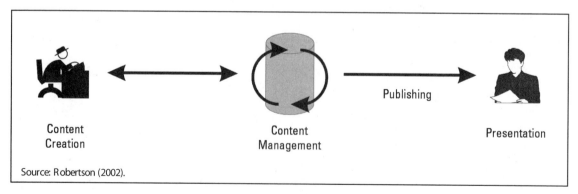

Content
Creation

Content
Management

Publishing

Presentation

Source: Robertson (2002).

and a description of the phases for content creation, content management, publishing options, and presentation of the information follows.

- *Content creation:* A CMS enables individuals to create content and provides a full range of features, including multi-user authoring, which provides version control and prevents authors from updating the same content at the same time; content reuse, in which a single page of content can be used in different contexts or provided to different users; and capturing metadata for tagging content with keywords for quicker searching capabilities.

- *Content management:* The key purpose of a CMS is content management—including version control, archiving, managing document workflows, security and audit trails, integration with external systems, and reporting. Version control enables only one version of a document to be updated at a time and provides legal accountability, backup, and disaster recovery capabilities. CMSs provide security levels so that authors having certain permissions can access only specific documents and audit trails indicating who last accessed and changed content, and what the changes were.

- *Publishing:* A CMS takes content stored in the repository and creates the final output based on the system capabilities and an individual's requirements. For example, some CMSs use stylesheets and page templates to create the output of content in a standard format, saving time for individuals who do not have to format the final content. CMSs can also publish content to multiple formats, including HTML (web), printed, PDF, and hand-held. For organizations with portals, individuals can have information from the CMS displayed in different ways based on the user profile of the individual.

- *Presentation:* Depending on the specifications designated during the system design and implementation phases, many CMSs enable individuals to view pages through Web browsers, navigate through the system and pages easily, and include search fields for quickly locating information based on keyword searches.

Learning Content Management Systems

As noted by Hall and Hall (2004), a learning content management system (LCMS) applies the primary functions of content management—storing, searching for, and reusing content—to the training development process. In an LCMS, content is chunked (typically into learning objects, which are small, reusable pieces of content) and then managed, published, and delivered on demand.

LCMSs integrate different courses and learning materials and package content for print, CD-ROM, or electronic publication, and most are capable of importing prepackaged content from other learning content development tools, such as Microsoft Word and Macromedia Dreamweaver. Most LCMSs enable course developers to author learning content. In addition, LCMSs allow developers to create and manage course content in a centralized way and to forgo hours of manual work, reuse and reconfigure already existing course content, and create multiple courses for multiple purposes, using the same content. While

LCMSs can integrate training content, they do not integrate with HR systems. Some LCMSs attempt this with course attendance, completions, and competencies.

The goal of an LCMS is to manage content in a highly accessible, automated database where the work of many training professionals is combined into one centralized hub, those who need to design a course from scratch, build a new course with existing content, or find chunks of knowledge or learning objects to plug into a course under development can do so in a flash. In short, LCMSs can make the most of existing content yet support rapid development of new content. Depending on the LCMS, many offer additional benefits, as summarized by Hall and Hall:

- *Faster development:* Most LCMSs offer a what-you-see-is-what-you-get (WYSIWYG) authoring environment, enabling WLP professionals to create and publish just-in-time training quickly.

- *Collaboration:* Storing learning content in an LCMS provides functions that surpass what typical learning authoring tools offer. Many LCMSs also have check-in and check-out capabilities that enable multiple users in different locations to access and work on the same course simultaneously. In addition, versioning features support collaborative efforts by offering quick and easy backups.

- *Reuse:* Searching capabilities allow WLP professionals to search for and reuse content. WLP professionals can also create the same content and publish it in multiple formats.

- *Quick global updates:* WLP professionals can access a learning object quickly and update it in one place, and when it's published, all instances of the object are updated in the system.

Portals

A web portal is a website that serves as a starting point to other resources on the Internet or an intranet. Intranet portals, also known as enterprise information portals, provide access to an array of resources and services, such as email, forums, search engines, and online shopping malls. The first web portals were online services, such as AOL. Today, many early search engines have changed into web portals to attract a larger audience. Many business portals offer collaboration services to share information in workplaces.

Enterprise Web Portals

As defined by Wikipedia, **Web portals** are sites on the World Wide Web that typically provide personalized capabilities to their visitors. They are designed to use distributed applications, different numbers and types of middleware (the software layer between the operating system and applications), and hardware to provide services from a number of different sources. In addition, business portals are designed to share collaboration in workplaces. A further business-driven requirement of portals is that the content be able to work on multiple platforms, such as personal computers, personal digital assistants (PDAs), and cell phones.

In the early 2000s, a major industry shift in web portal focus has been corporate intranet portals, or enterprise webs. Many organizations use private web portals to unite web communications and thinking within a large organization while saving money on labor and technology. Some corporate analysts have predicted that corporate intranet web portal spending will be one of the top five areas for growth in the Internet technologies sector during the first decade of the 21st century.

As noted by Wikipedia, some features of enterprise web portals follow.

- *Single touch point:* The portal becomes a delivery mechanism for all business information services.

- *Collaboration:* Portal members can communicate synchronously (through chat or messaging) or asynchronously through threaded discussions, email digests (forums), and blogs.

- *Content and document management:* The portal offers services that support the full life cycle of document creation and provide mechanisms for authoring, approval, version control, scheduled publishing, indexing, and searching.

- *Personalization:* This features allows portal members to subscribe to specific types of content and services. Users can customize the look and feel of their environment.

- *Integration:* Functions and data from multiple systems can be connected into new components or portlets.

Document Management Systems

As noted by Wikipedia, "originally, a document management system was a computer program (or set of programs) used to track and store images of paper documents. More recently, the term has been used to distinguish between imaging and records management systems that specialize in paper capture and records, respectively. Document management systems commonly offer check-in, check-out, storage, and retrieval of electronic documents. Electronic document management systems typically include a workflow model for certifying and electronically signing documents."

Collaboration Tools

Knowledge-sharing products help with collecting and exchanging information in an organization. Collaborative groupware products belong in this category. For example, the suite of Lotus Notes/Domino/Websphere applications is an example of a groupware product. Other products in this category, such as traditional search engines, help retrieve specific facts from a repository. An indexed search presupposes a conditioned repository of text. When using a search engine, users must begin with a known fact or keyword to start the search process—they know what they don't have.

According to Curtis J. Bonk, author of *Collaborative Tools for E-Learning* (2002), in today's society, the need for collaboration, communication, and conversation can lead to a competitive advantage. Collaborative technologies (also called **collaborative learning software**) have emerged as a way to familiarize learners with new expectations and experiences.

Collaboration tools include email, computer networks, whiteboards, bulletin board systems, chat rooms, and online presentation tools. These technologies play an important role in the expansion of e-learning and in collaborating on projects, sharing information, and communicating. Although one goal of e-learning is knowledge transfer, collaborative learning tools can also foster student analysis skills, critical thinking, and idea generation, and they can help bridge the gaps of perceived importance or practice.

Knowledge management isn't just for organizations; it's for everyone. New collaboration tools enable users to search for and organize documents and information on their desktops. For example, Groove offers collaboration tools and has both offline and cross-organizational capabilities. Some of these tools offer automated synchronization and version control for updating documentation. The following sections describe some categories of collaborative learning software in more detail.

Synchronous Collaboration Tools and Live Training

According to Bonk, that many collaborative tools—such as WebEx, PlaceWare, Horizon-Live, LearnLinc (Mentergy), Interwise, Centra, and NetMeeting—are often mentioned as synchronous WBT tools. In terms of common features and functions, synchronous Web-based collaboration platforms and tools typically include shared whiteboards and chat tools. For collaboration, chat tools nurture learner brainstorming and questioning, presenter clarifications and explanations, role play, and private one-to-one mentoring. They make it possible to collect immediate responses to an idea from learners around the globe. In addition, an electronic whiteboard can help focus learners on certain ideas or processes. Other common synchronous training tools are breakout rooms, online surveys or polling programs, file transfer programs, and discussion boards.

A key benefit of these tools includes promoting knowledge transfer through expert demonstrations or modeling and immediate learner application. Although there are often complaints about stability and fidelity of this training's video and audio elements, synchronous training is especially useful in sales training for new product announcements.

Conferencing Tools

Bonk points out, in addition to synchronous training, there are opportunities for collaboration in asynchronous learning environments. Many conferencing tools (for example, WebBoard, SiteScape Forum, FirstClass) allow learners to discuss topics at their leisure with no geographical or time zone restrictions on contributions. In fact, team meetings can take place across continents and over many time zones. For those who want to discuss issues in real time, conferencing tools often have synchronous chat options. Instructors or mentors can create online teams for small-group work or product development with the aid of conferencing tools that are embedded in LCMSs. Many synchronous tools allow the user to record the session, apply metatags to the content, and allow users to interact with it synchronously.

Requirements

When using technology to capture and facilitate organizational knowledge, organizations should consider these factors:

- Research and select technology that's well proven and suited to the defined tasks of knowledge management processes.

- Ensure that the technology provides consistent links to related subjects and make sure the links are maintained.

- Verify the ability to tailor the technology as closely as possible to the organization's learning environment.

- Research the open environment capabilities for Internet access, collaboration, and discussion tools.

- Confirm whether the technology allows electronic survey posting and data collection.

- Explore the ease of use of websites and the ability to tailor the technology to the organization's needs.

- Verify workflow capabilities and requirements of organizational processes and information highways. When possible, automate all forms and processes.

✓ **Chapter 6 Knowledge Check**

1. **Which of the following systems manages components that make up a course?**

   __ **A.** CMS

   __ **B.** LCMS

   __ **C.** LSS

   __ **D.** Collaboration tools

2. **A training manager is attempting to provide a tool that will allow employees to readily access small chunks of learning quickly and as frequently as needed. Which management system will best meet the training manager's needs?**

   __ **A.** RDBMS

   __ **B.** LCMS

   __ **C.** CMS

   __ **D.** PDF

3. **A training manager is working to deploy a series of PDFs and other critical information so that they are readily accessible to employees. Which management system best represents the needed solution?**

   __ **A.** RDBMS

   __ **B.** LCMS

   __ **C.** CMS

   __ **D.** PDF

4. **A training manager is working through the phases of content management. Which of the following is *not* considered a phase in the lifecycle of a content management system?**

   __ **A.** Creation

   __ **B.** Management

   __ **C.** Publishing

   __ **D.** Execution

5. **Which of the content management process phases helps to provide disaster recovery capabilities?**

   __ **A.** Content creation

   __ **B.** Content management

   __ **C.** Publishing

   __ **D.** Presentation

6. Which of the following includes email, computer networks, whiteboards, bulletin board systems, chat rooms, and online presentation tools, which play an important role in the expansion of e-learning and in collaborating on projects, sharing information, and communicating?

    __ **A.** CMS

    __ **B.** LCMS

    __ **C.** LSS

    __ **D.** Collaboration tools

7. A trainer has accessed her company's training site to make content additions and tweak user information. She has been enabled to do so by accessing

    __ **A.** Wikipedia

    __ **B.** A portal

    __ **C.** AOL

    __ **D.** A knowledge repository

8. A WLP professional is beginning work on a Six Sigma project and needs to access content specific to this topic. She enters her company's knowledge management intranet site and subscribes to several services that can continue to keep her updated on the topic. Which portal feature has she just benefited from?

    __ **A.** Single touch point

    __ **B.** Collaboration

    __ **C.** Personalization

    __ **D.** Integration

9. Document management systems accomplish all of the following *except*

    __ **A.** Check-in

    __ **B.** Check-out

    __ **C.** Storage

    __ **D.** Editing

10. A training manager is trying to retain information from old documents so that project teams have access to the legacy information. Which type of management system best meets this need?

    __ **A.** Content

    __ **B.** Learning

    __ **C.** Document

    __ **D.** Learning content

References

Bonk, C.J. (November 2002). "Collaborative Tools for E-Learning."

Chief Learning Officer: Solutions for Enterprise Productivity. Available at http://www. clomedia.com/content/templates/clo_feature.asp?articleid=41&zoneid=30.

Greenberg, L. (December 2002). "LMS and LCMS: What's the Difference?" *Learning Circuits.* Available at http://www.learningcircuits.org/2002/dec2002/greenberg.htm.

Hall, S.O., and B. Hall. (November 2004). "A Guide to Learning Content Management Systems." *Training.* pp. 33–37.

Harris, P.M., and O.S. Castillo. (2002). "Instructional Design for WBT." *Infoline* No. 250202.

Mantyla, K., and J.R. Gividen. (1997). *Distance Learning: A Step-by-Step Guide for Trainers.* Alexandria, VA: ASTD Press.

Newman, A. (1999). "Knowledge Management." *Infoline* No. 259903.

Robertson, J. (January 2002). "How to Evaluate a Content Management System." *KM Column.* Available at: http://www.steptwo.com.au/papers/kmc_evaluate/ pdf/ KMC_EvaluateCMS.pdf.

Wikipedia, the Free Encyclopedia. (2006). Wikimedia Foundation, Inc. Available at: http:/ /en.Wikipedia.org/wiki/Main_Page.

7
Information Architecture

When designing a system to support knowledge management, an information architecture must be developed to facilitate and promote information sharing. An organization's information architecture includes an end-to-end assessment and implementation of an organization's requirements, such as incorporating workflow and electronic forms, using collaboration tools, and, most important, designing and developing a database that can store this information.

After information is captured, database tools must be used for effective mining of information. These tools include tagging and indexing data so that users are able to search for and retrieve this stored knowledge on demand. Because some information changes constantly, version control mechanisms are essential to ensure the data's currency and relevancy. Authenticity of data is also relevant, as identifying the data's owner or author is helpful in identifying the data's primary function or target audience. Knowledge management tools are useful only if they are user friendly. In this respect, designing a user interface that's easy to use and aligned with users' skills sets is crucial to establishing widespread acceptance and use of knowledge management tools in an organization.

Examining the target audience of data is also useful in recognizing the data's intent. Although the data's basic structure may be straightforward, its purpose and utility may differ based on communities of practice, as one community may prioritize one data attribute above others based on their use. For instance, when a database is storing a picture file, one community may prioritize the picture's graphical image, whereas another group may be more concerned with the file size or its creation data. Advanced information architecture allows each group to retrieve their required attributes from the system by developing a multidimensional approach to knowledge management. This approach incorporates a user interface portal that permits easy data retrieval, a network infrastructure to seek data, and hardware and software systems to report statistics about data. By providing these perspectives, information architecture facilitates both horizontal and vertical collaboration among users.

Learning Objectives:

☑ List several considerations that WLP professionals should consider with regard to implementing collaboration tools within an organization.

☑ Define several strategies for capturing knowledge with regard to system architecture.

Overview

Information architecture is a description or design specification for how information should be treated and organized. In web design, the term describes organizing online content into categories and creating an interface for displaying those categories.

The Internet, intranets, and extranets have made information and knowledge available at any time, anywhere, and with few boundaries. When organizations first started intranet sites as early efforts to begin knowledge management, many of them posted volumes of information without much rhyme or reason. For many organizations, the result was chaos instead of facilitating information and knowledge sharing.

Internet, intranet, and extranet sites provide value only if employees can navigate to, search for, and access information efficiently. Information architecture makes this happen. Information architecture focuses on

- defining the mission and vision for the site
- determining what content and functionality are needed for the site
- identifying how learners will access information by defining organization, navigation, labeling, and search capabilities.

So how do organizations organize volumes of information? An information architect develops a site map, which is a blueprint for organizing information in the most logical manner possible, giving the information structure and hierarchy. An information architect is responsible for understanding and managing the overall knowledge structure and tagging system. When designing sites and tools, information architects also need to account for collaboration capabilities and knowledge bases.

Collaboration

Sharing information and knowledge can lead to the creation of new ideas and new knowledge to add value to an organization. This sharing of information is known as collaboration. A knowledge management system should include plenty of opportunities for people to interact with each other via discussion groups, email, instant messaging, communities of practice or knowledge exchanges, and so forth.

So what is collaboration? Todd R. Groff and Thomas P. Jones (2003) say that "Collaboration is usually the product of one or more common goals, values, needs, ideas, visions, or interests. Collaboration groups consist of formal or informal, often self-organized, groups of employees who possess complementary knowledge and share interest in particular problems, processes, or projects in their organization. Collaborative communication is a critical part of a good personal knowledge management strategy. It may take place between two people, one-one-one, and meetings or among people via phone, e-mail, newsletters, or a company whiteboard. Wherever ideas are, they grow."

Some key considerations for using collaboration to support knowledge management include

- For collaboration to work in the knowledge management process, employees must give support to others on the job.

- Employees need information instantly—what they need to know when they want it. For this reason, many collaboration and database tools just complement personal networks for employees seeking answers. No matter how robust the search function, an employee's network of human relationships often determines which knowledge he or she accesses. For example, employees commonly ask other people for information and ask to be directed to a specific point in a database for lessons or tools.

- Organizations using knowledge management processes need to be aware of how culture is shaped and formed and the effect on new technology.

- For employees and teams to collaborate and work together, teams often go through several stages of development, from norming through performing. When using collaboration tools, an organization needs to recognize how group norms and group dynamics relate to culture and how the technology will be used and encouraged to leverage in the organization.

- Experience shapes culture, and each culture is different. Depending on the approach used to introduce knowledge management, the organizational culture may embrace the change or promptly reject it.

- The culture of a country shapes and influences the culture in an organization.

Knowledge Bases

Organizing data and information so that workers can quickly enter, access, and retrieve information is crucial to the success of a knowledge management initiative. One tool, a knowledge base provides the access that employees need to seek and gain information and knowledge.

A knowledge base, as previously defined, is a specialized database that stores knowledge assets. Knowledge bases help employees access and share information to solve problems and increase the organization's collective knowledge. As noted by Rosenburg (2001), knowledge bases need to be created with logical links and tags between content elements and ensure that users get just enough information, just in time to meet their on-the-job information needs. The organization of information should make the level of detail in the knowledge base easy to discern and navigate—if users can't understand the information and how to easily access it, they won't use it.

When using knowledge management systems processes, some considerations for the nature and collection of knowledge include

- Decide how to capture and preserve expertise.

- Provide timely and up-to-date information to employees when and how they need it.

- Create knowledge maps to help users quickly navigate to and access information as needed.

- Structure knowledge storage, including hierarchies, taxonomies, and classification schemes. A taxonomy defines the rules and principles used to ensure consistent classification of data into ordered categories. For example, when creating a training document to support a sales organization, taxonomy rules might determine whether the document is saved to the training or sales category of the knowledge base.

- Metadata is information about content that enables it to be stored in and retrieved from a database. Metadata includes index fields used to hold unique data that identifies a record from all other records in the file or database. A metatag is an HTML tag identifying the contents of information on a website or in a knowledge base. Information commonly found in a metatag includes copyright information, keywords for search engines, and page formatting descriptions.

- Decide on entitlements and which employees should have access to which information.

- Decide on version control processes, how information gets updated, and procedures for checking out and checking in documents.

- Examine expiration procedures for documentation to ensure that outdated information is removed.

- Conduct user analysis and feedback to understand whether the system meets needs to access just-in-time information. The combination of menus, screen design, keyboard commands, online help, and so forth creates the way a learner interacts with a computer.

- Determine ownership and authorship of information.

Systems

Knowledge management is the explicit and systematic management of intellectual capital and the associated processes of creating, gathering, organizing, disseminating, leveraging, and using intellectual capital. On a fundamental level, knowledge management should be used when information and knowledge need to be in a readily accessible, tangible form for the purposes of sharing solutions and innovations, determining best practices, meeting customers' needs, improving responsiveness, and increasing collaboration.

The emergence of information technology has been the driving force behind many knowledge management initiatives. Systems are defined as a set of integrated components that function collectively to transform inputs into outputs for the purpose of achieving a common goal. When building and implementing systems to support knowledge management, development strategies must be linked to competencies.

Knowledge management can effectively transform an organization into one with a considerable competitive advantage; however, information technology shouldn't be the driving force behind a knowledge management initiative. Knowledge is not always the result when the desire to increase IT resources and uses is the key enabler behind the push for more information. Knowledge management requires more than intranets, databases, and the Internet; it often requires a shift in overall strategy.

Organizations also need to be aware of the organizational culture and whether employees are accustomed to using information to support and enhance job performance. Training and change management may be required to ensure that employees begin using the new knowledge management system and processes. This action helps organizations know whether the dollars invested in the knowledge management system actually provide value in the form of increased productivity and organizational learning.

✓ Chapter 7 Knowledge Check

1. A WLP professional is reviewing the information architecture for a system being built. The specifications include the mission and vision of the site and a description of how learners will access the system. The specifications also include the plan for navigation and search functions. The piece of the information architecture that appears to be missing is the type of RDBMS that will be used.

   ___ **A.** True

   ___ **B.** False

2. Collaborative communication is a critical part of a good personal knowledge management strategy.

   ___ **A.** True

   ___ **B.** False

3. A training manager has pulled information from the knowledge management system that describes copyright information and keywords for search engines. What information is he likely looking at?

   ___ **A.** HTML

   ___ **B.** Metatag

   ___ **C.** Taxonomy

   ___ **D.** RDBMS

4. A training manager is reviewing the key considerations when using collaboration to support knowledge management. Which of the following is *not* a key consideration?

   ___ **A.** Support among employees on the job

   ___ **B.** Instant access to information on the job

   ___ **C.** Version control procedures

   ___ **D.** The competitive landscape and how this tool can be compromised

5. Which of the following is best described as a system to help employees access and share information to solve problems and grow the collective knowledge of the organization?

   ___ **A.** Knowledge base

   ___ **B.** Knowledge management

   ___ **C.** Content management system

   ___ **D.** Learning content management system

6. **Which of the following is an HTML tag that includes copyright information, keywords for search engines, and page formatting descriptions?**

   __ **A.** Knowledge map

   __ **B.** Metatag

   __ **C.** Metadata

   __ **D.** Permissions

7. **When implementing a knowledge management system, all of the following are key considerations regarding the nature and collection of knowledge *except***

   __ **A.** Version control

   __ **B.** Metatagging

   __ **C.** Permissions

   __ **D.** Cost

8. **A WLP professional is working with her IT department to make certain that the sales management tool the client is using is effective and user friendly. What is the most important factor she should ensure about the tool?**

   __ **A.** Easy to access

   __ **B.** Converts old data

   __ **C.** It is collaborative

   __ **D.** Uses sales jargon

9. **A training manager is looking for a design specification on how the new knowledge management system will be constructed and how the data will be organized in the system. What term best describes what the manager is looking for?**

   __ **A.** Knowledge base

   __ **B.** Collaboration tools

   __ **C.** Information architecture

   __ **D.** Metadata

10. A training manager is reviewing several ways to capture information for a system architecture project. She notices that each week a group of project leads meet to discuss their projects and exchange ideas. The concept seems perfect for her project and so she decides to create the same type of group for her project. This type of strategy can best be considered as what type of knowledge capturing?

___ **A.** Metatags

___ **B.** Collaboration

___ **C.** Authorization

___ **D.** Groupthink

References

Garrett, J.J. (2002). "A Visual Vocabulary for Describing Information Architecture and Interaction Design." Available at http://www.jjg.net/ia/visvocab/.

Groff, T.R., and T.P. Jones. (2003). *Introduction to Knowledge Management.* Burlington, MA: Butterworth-Heinemann.

Langer, A.M. (2001). *Analysis and Design of Information Systems,* 2nd edition. New York: Springer-Verlag.

Marquardt, M. (1996). *Building the Learning Organization.* Alexandria, VA: ASTD Press.

Rosenburg, M. (2001). *E-Learning: Strategies for Delivering Knowledge in the Digital Age* . New York: McGraw-Hill.

Sanders, E.S., and S. Thaigarajan. (2001). *Performance Intervention Maps.* Alexandria, VA: ASTD Press.

Shiple, J. (2005). Information Architecture Tutorial. Available at http://webmonkey .wired. com/webmonkey/design/site_building/tutorials/tutorial1.html.

Vodvarka, J.A. "Information Architecture: Designing the User Experience." Available at http://web.archive.org/web/20010604212326/http://www.luminant.com/IMAGES/ WP_InformationArchitecture.pdf.

8
Database Management

A ***database management system (DBMS)*** is a collection of programs enabling the storage of information in a database. The primary goal of a DBMS is to provide a storage mechanism that can support efficient storage and retrieval of large amounts of data. Employees search for and access DBMS data to read information or, depending on their user permissions, modify and extract information.

To maintain a strategic knowledge management environment, an organization must maintain a database robust enough to handle its current and projected requirements. Incorporating a DBMS in the enterprise is essential for storing and retrieving large amounts of data, including its unique attributes. Relational databases have become the industry standard because they offer multidimensional views of data based on complex relationships between key elements. Key characteristics of a robust DBMS include querying to permit data retrieval, indexing to expedite the retrieval process, and tuning tools to enhance performance. To ensure that a DBMS can support the information infrastructure's capabilities, a knowledge database manager should be consulted.

Learning Objectives:

- ☑ Define the purpose of a database management system.

- ☑ Describe two types of database server platforms and features.

- ☑ Identify the importance of query generation with regard to a knowledge management system.

- ☑ Explain the importance of other support requirements with regard to knowledge management systems, including specialists, performance testing, back-up facilities, and the ability to support specific formats.

Database Server Platforms

Databases enable users to store, manage, and retrieve information through the use of tables. These tables are similar to spreadsheet applications, in that data is organized into columns and rows. Each row of data in a database represents a record, and each record must have at least one unique identifier, known as the primary key, to distinguish one row of data from all other data. However, databases have much more power and functionality than spreadsheets. For example, many spreadsheet applications can store only up to 65,500 rows of data, but databases don't have this limitation. In addition, databases offer the following features:

- *Ability to retrieve all information matching specific criteria entered via a query:* For example, the official name of a course has changed and the database information needs to be updated. A query, or question, is entered to access the current course name and information in the database.

- *Quick mass updates of records in the database:* For example, the name of an upcoming course has been modified. Currently, 120 employees are scheduled to take the course in the next quarter. By updating the course name in one table, all records indicating that employees are scheduled to take the course are updated as well.

- *Ability to cross-reference and link to records in other tables in the database:* For example, employee records may also be linked to a training records table to enable WLP and HRD professionals to see courses that employees have taken or are scheduled to take in accordance with their professional development plan.

- *Perform complex summing and other calculations:* For example, at the end of the year, a WLP professional wants to pull a list of each class that was offered, sum the number of students and number of classes that occurred during the year, calculate the average number of students per class, and calculate the average cost per student to provide the instruction.

Types of Database Server Platforms

DBMSs range in size from small desktop database applications to large systems that process all the data for an organization. IT professionals are often faced with the challenge of selecting an appropriate database platform for a project or an organization. After selecting a database server platform, the next decision is how to organize information in the database. Some options include relational, network (lattice-style), flat, and hierarchical (tree-style) structures. The internal organization of data affects the system's performance and user satisfaction; for example, if data access is slow and finding information with a search is difficult, the investment in the DBMS may not result in the expected ROI.

After the needs analysis supplies answers to key questions, the process of evaluating specific DBMSs can begin. The first consideration is selecting the DBMS and database server platform. There are two categories of DBMSs—relational databases and multidimensional or column-oriented databases.

A **_relational database management system (RDBMS_**) stores data in the form of tables linked by a unique identifier. These relationships provide the power behind RDBMSs because they require few assumptions as to how data is linked and related. Even though data is stored in many different tables, relational databases make it easy to work with individual records for updating. When users query the database, database information can be viewed in many different ways.

In a **_flat file database,_** all data is contained in one table, as opposed to a **_multidimensional database (MDB)._** MDBs are often generated from relational databases and designed to optimize analytical processing. They are frequently used for data warehousing and online analytical processing (OLAP) needs. MDBs process data and provide answers to queries quickly.

Many installations use a combination of the two, storing detailed data in a relational database and using an MDB for certain data marts with well-known analysis patterns. A **_data mart_** is a specialized version of a data warehouse that provides insight into operational data, such as trends that enable management to make strategic decisions.

Selecting a Database Server Platform

Selecting a database platform for an organization can seem like an unwieldy task. IT professionals need to perform a comprehensive needs analysis to identify business and user requirements—as well as any unknown requirements that will affect the database selection, scale considerations, and implementation requirements and timeline. The needs analysis team should be similar to a joint application development (JAD) team used for any other IT implementation. Typically, JAD teams include a project sponsor; a project manager; IT personnel responsible for designing, developing, customizing, and deploying the DBMS; and a group of end users who will use the system to access information needed on the job.

As Chapple (2004) points out, a needs analysis should answer the following questions:

- Who will be using the database, and what tasks will they perform?

- How often will data be modified and who will make the modifications?

- Who will provide IT support for the DBMS?

- What hardware will be available, and is a budget for additional hardware available?

- Who will be responsible for maintaining data?

- Will data access be offered over the Internet? If so, what level of access and permissions should be granted?

Query Generation

Users can enter requests for information from a database in the form of a *query* or question. The structure for constructing a query is known as a query language. Different DBMSs support different query languages. Structured Query Language (SQL) is often the standard query language and defines all user and administrator interactions. Many databases have a user-friendly graphical user interface (GUI), but behind the scenes, SQL is interpreting mouse clicks and carrying out commands.

DMBSs support the type of queries generated by a suite of *business intelligence (BI)* tools—the tools and systems that play a role in strategic planning—that help organizations make decisions. The properties of these tools often include sophisticated optimization, query parallelism, mechanisms to partition large tables, and resource governors.

Support Specialists

After the platform and DBMS are selected, IT support is crucial to maximize an organization's technology investment. A team of experts should be selected early in the process to participate on the project team. Before system implementation, the people responsible for ongoing maintenance and support of the DBMS should be identified. If they aren't the same people as those participating on the project team during the design and implementation phases, a turnkey transition plan should be created to formally transfer information, knowledge and responsibility from design specialists to the ongoing support specialists. Depending on the type of DBMS that's chosen, a highly skilled and knowledgeable group of IT professionals may be needed to ensure its ongoing performance.

Performance Testing

Before using a new DBMS, the implementation team must plan for ample time to allow performance prototyping during the design phase. Since experts even run into problems for IT implementations, it's not unusual to have a lengthy prototype testing timeline to deal with unexpected performance problems, such as workload and process optimization.

Support for Specific Formats

IT professionals need to determine whether BI or knowledge management activities will involve the analysis of unstructured large objects, such as text documents or images. For example, a DBMS may include text and other information; however, large objects may be stored—and, therefore, need to be managed—outside the DBMS. If an organization decides to store large objects in an RDBMS, certain processes, such as logging—controlling how the computer collects and analyzes data—may be optional or prohibited for objects over a certain size.

Back-up Facilities and Fall-Back Procedures

If problems with the DBMS do occur, IT professionals need to plan for the backup and recovery of database information. Many databases store certain types of data but also link to data outside the DBMS, such as graphics. For items that aren't stored in the DBMS, a back-up plan must be created for data and BI information or activities that aren't part of the system. IT professionals need to select and design the physical data storage mechanisms during the database design phase.

✓ Chapter 8 Knowledge Check

1. **The purpose of a DBMS is to provide a storage mechanism that can support efficient storage and retrieval of large amounts of data.**

   __ **A.** True

   __ **B.** False

2. **Databases offer all of the following features *except***

   __ **A.** Quick mass updates of records in the database

   __ **B.** Ability to retrieve all information matching specific criteria entered via a query

   __ **C.** Ability to share information and knowledge, leading to the creation of new ideas and new knowledge

   __ **D.** Perform complex summing and other calculations

3. **What kind of database makes it easy to work with individual records for updating, but also enables users to view database information in many different ways?**

   __ **A.** Relational database

   __ **B.** Flat file database

   __ **C.** Multidimensional database

   __ **D.** Data mart

4. **Many database installations may use a combination of two databases, for example relational and multidimensional.**

   __ **A.** True

   __ **B.** False

5. **A training manager is requiring that the database back end to his learning management system be very powerful and able to link data across several tables of information about courses, resources, and employees taking training. What would be the best type of database to support this type of application?**

   __ **A.** Multidimensional

   __ **B.** Relational

   __ **C.** Flat file

   __ **D.** Data mart

6. **The questions that individuals can pose when searching a database take the form of search statements.**

   __ **A.** True

   __ **B.** False

7. **A training manager is looking to house a collection of tools and systems that play a role in strategic planning to help the training unit make decisions. What type of tool is the training manager looking for?**

   __ **A.** Business intelligence tools

   __ **B.** SQL

   __ **C.** Collaboration tools

   __ **D.** RDBMSs

8. **Performance testing for a knowledge management system is important because in any system implementation there are going to be unexpected performance problems that must be tested before the system "goes live."**

   __ **A.** True

   __ **B.** False

9. **A WLP professional has been alerted to large files requiring organizing in the database management system. What support is likely needed for this issue?**

   __ **A.** A backup plan

   __ **B.** A needs analysis to identify business and user requirements

   __ **C.** Analysis of unstructured objects

   __ **D.** Performance testing

10. **A WLP professional is attempting to pull together a resource team to support the implementation of the knowledge management system. Which of the following factors is *not* considered part of an RDBMS?**

    __ **A.** Performance testing

    __ **B.** Support of data formats

    __ **C.** Back-up facilities

    __ **D.** Flat file creations

References

Butler, S. (September 1999). "Knowledge Management Directions: Database Management Considerations for BI and KM." Available at: http://dmreview.com/article_sub.cfm?articleId=1355.

Chapple, M. (October 2004). "Database Fundamentals." Available at http://databases.about.com/od/administration/a/databasefund.htm.

———. "Choosing a Database Product." Available at http://databases.about.com/od/administration/a/choosing.htm.

Cross, R., and L. Baird. (Spring 2000). "Technology is Not Enough: Improving Performance by Building Organizational Memory." *Sloan Management Review,* pp. 69–77.

National Institute of Open Schooling. (Accessed February 2006). "Lesson 29: Introduction to System Design and Analysis." Available at http://www.nos.org/htm/sad1.htm.

Webopedia: Online Computer Dictionary for Computer and Internet Terms and Definitions. (2006). Jupitermedia Corporation. Available at http://www. webopedia.com.

Wikipedia, the Free Encyclopedia. (2005). Wikimedia Foundation. Available at http://en.wikipedia.org/wiki/Main_Page.

9
System Analysis and Design

To accurately capture the requirements for developing a comprehensive and holistic knowledge management system, a rigorous system analysis and design must be conducted to look at the current system functionality (if it exists) and determine what deficiencies (or gaps) exist that would prohibit an organization from reaching its knowledge management goals. If the goals aren't met in the current system, a system specification should be designed that minimizes gaps between the current state and the desired state. The gap reduction may come from making modifications to the existing system or instituting a new system. In this manner, the business process analysis helps determine which system functions should be implemented and their priority for completion.

Learning Objective:

☑ List several techniques for developing systems and mapping workflow processes for systems.

Standard Techniques for Developing Systems

A system is a collection of components that, although they're independent, work together. The IPO (Input/Process/Output) model refers to systems for transforming data and information. Examples include technological innovations, such as voice and handwriting recognition systems and computer touch pads. As interventions, these systems help people improve their performance through the use of devices that facilitate and adapt work processes to individual needs and preferences. The IPO model functions within a project management framework to plan and assign the work to be accomplished on time, within budget, and within scope. Project management principles are the foundation for successfully completing a project through the processes of planning, organizing, and managing tasks, based on the elements of time, money, and available resources.

As defined in Chapter 5, the project life cycle is everything that happens from the beginning to the end of the project. Organizations usually divide projects into several project phases to better manage and control the project work. By managing projects in phases, project managers focus their time and energy on managing the current work but also look ahead to future phases. Collectively, the project phases are known as the project life cycle.

A *system development life cycle* is an organizational process of developing and maintaining systems. It helps in establishing a system project plan and lists the processes and subprocesses required to develop a system. The following list describes the phases in a system development life cycle (see Figure 9-1):

Figure 9-1. System Development Life Cycle and Phases

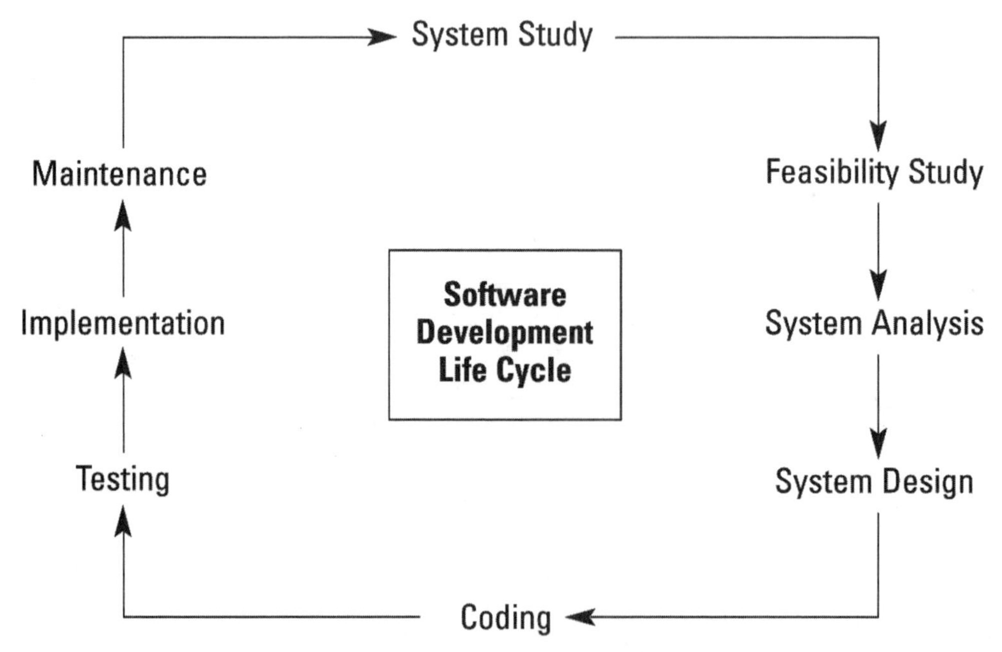

Source: National Institute of Open Schooling. "Lesson 29: Introduction to System Design and Analysis."

- *System study:* The first phase is conducted in two stages—the preliminary survey (defines the system scope) and a detailed analysis to identify user requirements and any limitations or problems in an existing system. The system study defines what the system should be and results in a system proposal documenting any limitations of the current system based on user requirements. This proposal should include problem identification, project initiation, background analysis, and inferences or findings.

- *Feasibility study:* This phase, conducted to identify the scope of the system development process, tests the proposal for the ability to meet user requirements, the cost-benefit ratio of developing the system or making changes, and resource requirements in terms of people, time, and cost.

- *System analysis:* If the project is approved, system analysis leverages the system study's findings to create detailed specifications for the new system. During this phase, data is collected with a variety of methods, including historical documentation, current system transactions and processes, interviews, observations, and questionnaires. System analysis focuses on new requirements, identified problems or risks, and tradeoffs in features to add versus the time, resource availability, and cost to make the changes. Detailed data flowcharts, data dictionaries, specifications, and logical data structures are usually outputs of this phase.

- *System design:* With the input of user requirements and a detailed analysis of the new system completed, the system design phase begins. This phase results in the creation of two deliverables: a preliminary or general design, which details the new system's features and their cost, and the structure or detailed design—the blueprint of a computer system, including input, output, and processing specifications. Some tools used in this phase include flowcharts, data flow diagrams, data dictionaries, decision tables, and decision trees.

- *Coding:* This phase requires converting the blueprint by entering the computer programming language to create the new system. At this point, the defined procedures in the documentation are translated into control specifications and computer instructions to indicate data movement and control of the entire system.

- *Testing:* A test run of the system uses a set of data to run through the system and check for bugs. The test run results should match the specifications and defined requirements for the output. Two types of tests may be run at this point. **Unit tests** are conducted in real working conditions using *test* data. Any errors must be noted and corrected. **System tests** are conducted with *real* data. If the outputs of the test don't match the specifications, errors are identified and corrected. This phase confirms user acceptance before the next phase can begin.

- *Implementation:* After user acceptance, this phase focuses on turning theory into practice. The system is installed on user computers and training ensues, based on the learning objectives outlined for what learners know.

- *Maintenance:* This phase is an ongoing process to eliminate errors in the system and to identify and reduce any variations in system output compared to the specifications.

If business, competitor, or other factors require a change in the system, the system development life cycle begins again with a system study to identify required changes.

Mapping Workflow Processes for Systems

For additional information on mapping workflow processes, see Chapter 5, "Business Process Analysis."

✓ Chapter 9 Knowledge Check

1. **One technique used to map work process flow includes the input-analysis-output model.**

   __ **A.** True

   __ **B.** False

2. **All of the following are standard phases in a system life cycle *except***

   __ **A.** Feasibility study

   __ **B.** Coding

   __ **C.** Communication

   __ **D.** System analysis

3. **Each phase of a project has one primary deliverable.**

   __ **A.** True

   __ **B.** False

4. **The testing phase of a systems implementation often includes two types—one with test data and one with real data.**

   __ **A.** True

   __ **B.** False

5. **Which of the following systems implementation phases requires converting the blueprint of the system into computer programming language?**

   __ **A.** Feasibility study

   __ **B.** Coding

   __ **C.** Testing

   __ **D.** System analysis

6. **The IPO model functions within a project management framework**

   __ **A.** True

   __ **B.** False

7. **A WLP professional is working with the software creation team and has been notified that the team is in the coding stage of the cycle. Based on your knowledge of how system development works, what stage in the cycle happens next?**

__ **A.** Implementation

__ **B.** Maintenance

__ **C.** System analysis

__ **D.** System study

8. **Collectively, all phases of a project are known as the**

__ **A.** Product life cycle

__ **B.** Project scope

__ **C.** Project life cycle

__ **D.** Systems development life cycle

9. **The maintenance phase focuses on eliminating errors in the system and to identify and reduce variations.**

__ **A.** True

__ **B.** False

References

Groff, T.R., and T.P. Jones. (2003). *Introduction to Knowledge Management.* Burlington, MA: Butterworth-Heinemann.

National Institute of Open Schooling. (Accessed February 2006). "Lesson 29: Introduction to System Design and Analysis." Available at http://www.nos.org/htm/sad1.htm.

Rosenburg, M. (2001). *E-Learning: Strategies for Delivering Knowledge in the Digital Age.* New York: McGraw-Hill.

Thompson, C. (1990). "Project Management: A Guide." *Infoline* No. 259004.

Waagen, A.K. (1998). "Task Analysis." *Infoline* No. 259808.

10
Strategies to Manage Culture Change

 The one true absolute in life is that change will happen. With the speed of technological improvements and changes, organizations are struggling to keep up with innovations, competition, technology, and transformed employees. Managing these culture changes has become one of the biggest challenges facing organizations.

Knowledge management is essential for managing change. Communicating with employees and customers makes the change process move forward smoothly. Today's employees may have a different work ethic than that of employees in the past, but they are still committed to their organizations. They have expectations that organizational leaders need to address. They are likely skilled at technology and comfortable with rapid changes. They expect to have ample communication and be part of strategic goals. Business executives and managers need to use this knowledge expectation to help them meet strategic goals and adjust to change.

Every organization has a set of values, morals, and norms. Cultural views are based on demographics, historical context, and economic traditions. Changing employees' views or attitudes is difficult. Through knowledge sharing, open discussion, and up-to-date information, employees can feel as though they're part of an organization's strategic goals. When employees are part of the change, they're more likely to embrace it. Leadership should be careful not to make major changes to policy or process without input from members of the organization. Although the successful outcome of strategic goals is linked to fiscal success, culture changes affect the outcome more.

Organizations need to identify people in the organization who influence others. These key players, who are found at any level in the organization, can make or break an organization. Communicating and involving these employees in strategic goals improve the chances of successful change.

By understanding organizational culture, its symbols and hidden meanings, its values, and its underlying assumptions, managers can change—or at least manipulate—culture, and in so doing, change the behavior of workers.

Learning Objective:

☑ Describe the importance of managing culture change with regard to knowledge management and two characteristics that established cultures share.

Key Knowledge: Strategies to Manage Culture Change

Training has a specific role in maintaining or manipulating culture: Many corporate values and beliefs are disseminated through training and orientation programs and in socialization systems, in which new employees are introduced to the organization's culture.

Established cultures provide common ideas that help people cope—both individually and as a group—with life's ambiguities. According to Harrison Trice and Hanice Neyer (1993), authors of *The Cultures of Work Organizations*, established cultures share these major characteristics:

- *Collectiveness:* Cultures reflect the commonly held beliefs of their members. Those who fail to endorse and practice a culture's prevailing beliefs, values, and norms are marginalized and may be punished or expelled.

- *Emotionally charged:* Because cultures evolve to help deal with anxiety, they are infused with both emotion and meaning. "People cherish and cling to established ideologies because they seem to make the future predictable by making it conform to the past," Trice and Neyer note.

- *Historically based:* A specific culture results from the unique history of a group coping with a special set of physical, social, political, and economic circumstances. "Cultures cannot be divorced from their histories and they do not arise overnight," Trice and Neyer stress.

- *Inherently symbolic:* Symbolism—things representing other things—plays an important role in cultures. "Symbols are the most general and pervasive of cultural forms," say Trice and Neyer.

- *Dynamic:* Cultures, although they're passed from generation to generation and create continuity, are changing constantly.

- *Vagueness:* Cultures "incorporate contradictions, ambiguities, paradoxes, and just plain confusion," Trice and Neyer state. Cultures may have both central and peripheral elements. Fuzziness marks the peripheries and might represent miscommunications, sub- and counterculture influence, or changing circumstances.

"An organization's decision to change its culture is generally triggered by a specific event or situation," according to a U.S. Government Accounting Office study. These events or situations range from international competition to severe budget restrictions.

For more information, see Module 5, *Facilitating Organizational Change*, Chapter 5, "Organizational Systems, Culture, and Political Dynamics."

11
Adult Learning Theory

 Adult learning theories are based on psychological, sociological, and adult continuing education concepts. A learning theory identifies the processes, causes, and responses to learning as identified by a group of people. Learning theories explain how people learn as well as why they learn. Concrete, visual, and auditory learners learn by direct contact and experience, so hands-on learning is beneficial for them. Abstract, reflective, or book learners learn through new information, analysis, and reflection. Study and book review is beneficial for these learners.

Learning occurs with observation, return demonstration, or interest in a subject, and reward or punishment can direct learning. These are examples of how adults learn but more vital to organizational learning is why they learn. Most commonly used in the workplace, the classroom setting is successful at offering information to a large number of people but has little effect on changing work activities or imparting new information. Lecture is the least effective method for learning. Change occurs when an adult identifies a need for the change. How people learn, where they are learning, and why they are learning are key factors in adult learning. Adults in a work setting are expected to already have a set of skills and knowledge. An organization can improve its strategic goals, promote employee satisfaction, and increase customer satisfaction by providing education to the right people via the right method. New information can be shared at department levels. Organizational goals should be shared, and ideas from employees encouraged. Mentoring and modeling in the organization are vital to change and allow a flow of information from employees to top management. Learning can take place when communication is open. The questions an organization needs to ask are "What information needs to be shared with employees?" "How do we effectively share this information?" and "What do employees need?"

Just as important is the historical context of the employee. Educators must understand employees' background, education, and what the organization has taught them indirectly about the need to learn. If the organization has a history of spitting out information and asking employees to spit it back, little learning will take place. Teaching is not the ultimate goal. An employee's desire to learn and relearn is the ultimate goal of sharing knowledge.

Learning Objective:

☑ Summarize several key concepts of how adults learn and the importance of creating an environment for learning.

Key Knowledge: Principles of Adult Learning

Seven key principles summarize how adults learn:

Adult learning is andragog: **Andragogy,** a term coined by Malcolm Knowles (1988), refers to the art and process of teaching adults. Andragogy encompasses principles that instructional designers must address when preparing learning programs for adults. **Pedagogy,** however, refers to the art and science of teaching children, whose learning needs differ significantly from those of adults.

Adult learners are pressed for time: Adults squeeze learning in between demanding jobs, family responsibilities, and community commitments. Even when they are highly motivated to learn, the call of life limits the time many adults can invest in learning.

Adult learners are goal oriented: Adults primarily participate in learning programs to achieve a particular goal. The goal may be work related, such as using a computer system more effectively, or personal, such as learning Japanese before a vacation.

Adult learners bring previous knowledge and experience: When possible, linking new course material to learners' existing knowledge and experience creates a powerful, relevant learning experience. Sometimes, however, content in a program contradicts material that people have learned previously. In these situations, designers of training programs must first convince learners to part with the old approach so that they can grasp the new.

Adult learners have a finite interest in types of information: Although many training courses tackle complex topics, most learners are primarily interested in aspects of the content that affect them directly. In many cases, that's just a small part of the content. When learners see limited application of the additional content, they absorb little of it, sometimes tuning out the content that does affect them.

Adult learners have different motivation levels: During the first six to 12 weeks on the job, adults are highly motivated to learn. When faced with new work processes or approaches, adults are similarly motivated to learn. (Fear of failure and difficulty of unlearning old habits, however, might stifle their motivation at this point.) As they become more familiar with the content, learners' motivation to learn wanes until a specific need arises.

Adult learners have different learning styles: **Learning style** refers to how a person prefers to pick up new content. Each person has a number of preferred learning styles.

For more information see Module 1, *Designing Learning,* Chapter 1, "Cognition and Adult Learning Theory."

12
After Action Review Methodology

Measurement can identify outcomes or provide information that will allow for potential improvement for organizations, departments, and individuals. Analyzing the actions that occurred becomes a learning process and a way to capture issues, identify problems, and document successful solutions. Issues can occur at various levels in an organization including individual, customer, or organizational. Some key questions that should be asked include "Do employees have the tools and the skills to do what they need to do?" and "Are departments sharing information with those who could use it?"

To measure for improvement, an organization must have a process. Most common is a process that identifies four areas to assess change:

- Problem identification (may be of high risk to the organization, low risk but a frequent problem, new to the organization, or identified by problem analysis)

- Identify possible solutions/people involved

- Initiate a plan for knowledge sharing

- Evaluate success (may be used in measuring large projects or small issues in an organization; a measurement usually includes a percentage of desired improvement).

While there are many evaluation and improvement methods that organizations can employ, After Action Review (AAR) is highlighted in this section as one of those possible methods.

Learning Objectives:

☑ Describe the purpose and benefits of AARs.

☑ Discuss how AARs can serve as a measurement for improvement and the importance of defining metrics and capturing lessons learned.

Measurement of Improvement

Employees should learn from experience in ways that benefit the organization's future and their current projects. Companies need to maximize individual learning and then make that learning available to other employees.

The U.S. Army was the first large entity to use *After Action Reviews (AARs)*. In the U.S. Army and other organizations, AARs have proved to be an effective, structured way to get people to capture learning from their experiences. The U.S. Army used AARs to identify the original intent of a mission, what went right and wrong, and what factors affected the mission and the situations presented.

According to Wiig (2004), the key purpose and benefits of AARs include

- improving the accuracy and detail of feedback available to management and employees
- identifying collective and individual strengths and how to leverage them
- identifying collective and individual deficiencies and how to correct them
- reinforcing and increasing the learning that took place during a business activity
- increasing interest and motivation
- guiding individuals and groups toward achieving performance objectives
- identifying lessons learned so that they can be applied to subsequent activities or tasks
- increasing confidence in performing capability
- increasing the proficiency of all participants.

Many organizations use AARs to continually improve new product development and internal processes. According to Cross and Baird (2000), Analog Devices uses AARs as product development teams work on one project with many interrelated tasks.

In this process, team members summarize what happened in a one-page document. Other team members later review this document and identify what was learned and how that knowledge can be used to improve processes, products, and performance.

The one-page summaries are then compiled and used during a six-week review of all product development projects. As noted by Cross and Baird, "Team learning is gathered and then used to modify processes in an effort to improve the product development process itself. Although it might seem the process stops there, that's not the case at Analog Devices. The six-week reviews become the basis for a total review when the organization introduces new products into the marketplace."

Cross and Baird outline a process by five questions to enable teams and individuals to analyze what happened during these reviews. The process includes

- *What was the intent?* What was the purpose of the action and what was the group or person trying to accomplish? In describing and evaluating the intent, be as specific as possible.

- *What happened?* What exactly occurred? Why? Why not? What were the results? Because recalling accurately what happened may be hard, conducting an AAR as soon after the event as possible is crucial.

- *What was learned?* On the basis of what the group or person tried to do and what actually happened, what was learned? What does the group or person know now that they didn't know before they started? If someone else were to start down the same path, what advice would the group or person give this person?

- *What does the group or person do now?* Based on what's known now, what should the group or person do? Because the focus of an AAR is on action, focusing on learning that can be applied to the action quickly is important.

- *Who else should be told?* Who else needs to know what has been learned? What do they need to know? How should the information be communicated? How can the group or person leverage what was learned to drive organization-wide performance?

Lessons Learned

When implementing a knowledge management system to support existing work and capture new knowledge, these systems include procedures for gathering information from employees directly involved when notable situations occur. According to Karl M. Wiig, lessons learned may include solved problems, how a mishap was prevented, a recognized opportunity, and so on. Lessons learned procedures require quick assembly of participants to capture all relevant information, often in a defined, structured format to make the knowledge available when it's needed.

A sample process for capturing lessons learned may include

1. identification of the people involved in the lesson learned
2. procedures for the capture process
3. repository for initial, unedited captured information
4. editing process
5. approval process for including the lesson learned into the final knowledge base.

At the end of this process, the knowledge base is updated with all lessons learned.

Metrics for Usage and Value

As mentioned previously, every process needs to have a measurement process. An example of a measurement process is 64 percent of employees attending safety education—the goal is 100 percent. By identifying and carrying out a solution, the percentage should change. Not every problem has an attached percentage, however. Many initiatives are measured successfully if the problem no longer occurs over a number of weeks or months. Graphs, pie charts, and other methods are appropriate to use when graphing results of the measurement. Table 12-1 shows an example of a measurement tool.

Measurement and improvement help the bottom line but shouldn't be the most important factors in knowledge management. Successful organizations recognize that employees want to do things well, but often employers don't provide the tools, knowledge, and time. Employees who have a voice and receive feedback and rewards can be advocates for their organizations. Measurement should be used to assist employees in achieving goals they share with the organization.

Table 12-1. Sample Measurement Tool

Process Step	Description
Problem	Require 100 percent attendance at training; 64 percent attendance is the current metric.
Analysis	Determine why attendance is low: for example, the inability to have more than two employees in each department training at one time, or employees may have heavy travel schedules that do not coincide with training schedules.
Solutions	Increase the number of services and provide makeup dates and packets.
Implement/Action	Provide three extra in-services, including production and distribution of packets. Require a one-month advance return of registrations. Notify managers of registrations and noncompliance.
Result	All staff complete training.
Final analysis	Continue strategies and processes to drive 100 percent attendance change and evaluate the process again next year.

✓ Chapter 12 Knowledge Check

1. **Which of the following best describes why measuring an organization's knowledge management initiative is important?**

    __ **A.** Measurement requires strong statistical controls and, therefore, provides valid and reliable data.

    __ **B.** Measurement involves everyone in the organization.

    __ **C.** Measurement is the only way an organization, a department, or a person can assess outcomes or potential improvement.

    __ **D.** Measurement provides an initial benchmark.

2. **The purpose of after action reviews in many organizations is to continually identify which content needs to be updated in the knowledge management system.**

    __ **A.** True

    __ **B.** False

3. **After action reviews use a series of questions to facilitate the discussion and review process.**

    __ **A.** True

    __ **B.** False

4. **Which of the following terms describes the type of information captured that may have been used to solve problems, discover how mishaps were prevented, or recognize opportunities?**

    __ **A.** Knowledge repository

    __ **B.** Tacit knowledge

    __ **C.** Knowledge exchange

    __ **D.** Lessons learned

5. **AARs were first conducted by the U.S. Army as a structured way to get people to capture their learning and experiences.**

    __ **A.** True

    __ **B.** False

6. **An AAR is one formal method of**

  __ **A.** Resource allocation

  __ **B.** Project planning

  __ **C.** System development

  __ **D.** Knowledge management

---

7. **A training manager is selling his management team on using AARs for their key projects. The management team thinks it is a waste of time and resources to do this task. What key point would be helpful to persuade the management team to conduct AARs in the future?**

  __ **A.** The identification of lessons learned can help other groups save time

  __ **B.** The interest and motivation of people in a project is increased

  __ **C.** The communication that results from this process is professional looking

  __ **D.** The U.S. Army does this and appears to have great success with the model

References

Cross, R., and L. Baird. (Spring 2000). "Technology is Not Enough: Improving Performance by Building Organizational Memory." *Sloan Management Review.* pp. 69–78.

Marquardt, M. (1999). *Action Learning in Action.* Palo Alto, CA: Davies-Black Publishing.

———. (1996). *Building the Learning Organization.* New York: McGraw Hill.

———. (2004). *Optimizing the Power of Action Learning.* Palo Alto, CA: Davies-Black Publishing.

Wiig, K.M. (2004). *People-Focused Knowledge Management: How Effective Decision Making Leads to Corporate Success.* Jordan Hill, Oxford: Elservier Butterworth-Heinemann.

Appendix A
Glossary

AAR (After Action Review) was first developed by the U.S. army and used in the military to focus on performance improvement and allow individuals to learn for themselves what happened, why, and how to improve performance.

Adult Learning Theory is a term that encompasses the collective theories and principles of how adults learn and acquire knowledge. Popularized by Malcolm Knowles, adult learning theory provides the foundation that WPL professionals need to meet workplace learning needs.

Andragogy (from the Greek meaning "adult learning") is the adult learning theory popularized by Malcolm Knowles, based on five key principles that influence how adults learn: self-concept, prior experience, readiness to learn, orientation to learning, and motivation to learn.

Best Practices are techniques that are believed to constitute a paradigm of excellence in a particular field.

Business Intelligence (BI) Tools are the tools and systems that play a role in strategic planning and help organizations make decisions.

Business Process Analysis is a structured method of documenting business rules and functions to uncover hidden inefficiencies that highlight strengths that could be streamlined or leveraged to increase productivity.

Business Process is how people, materials, methods, machines, and the environment combine to add value to a product or service. Everything that gets done is a part of the process—how the work gets done, roles and responsibilities, and resources and systems.

CMS (Content Management System) is a computer software system for organizing and facilitating collaborative creation of documents and other content. A content management system is frequently a web application used for managing websites and web content, though in many cases, content management systems require special client software for editing and constructing articles.

Collaborative Learning is an instructional approach in which learners and instructors share the responsibility for learning and work together to determine how the session should progress.

Community of Practice is a group of people who share a common interest in an area of competence and are willing to share the experiences of their practice.

Data Mart is a specialized version of a data warehouse that provides insight into operational data, such as trends that enable management to make strategic decisions.

DBMS (Database Management System) is software or a collection of software that enables users to access and manipulate data.

DMAIC (Define, Measure, Analyze, Improve, and Control) Methodology is a five-step process used for reduction of defects, process improvement, and customer satisfaction.

ECM (Enterprise Content Management) is a widely recognized IT term for software that enables organizations to create/capture, manage/secure, store/retain/destroy, publish/distribute, search, personalize, and present/view/print digital content.

EPSS (Electronic Performance Support System) is a computer application that's linked directly to another application to train or guide workers through completing a task in the target application. More generally, it is a computer or other device that gives workers information or resources to help them accomplish a task or achieve performance requirements. These systems deliver information on the job, just in time, and with minimum staff support.

Explicit is a type of knowledge includes information that has been documented or can be shared with someone.

Extranet is a private network that is similar to an intranet but does not include a firewall. This enables accessibility by outside companies or businesses through usernames and passwords.

Flat File Database is a database in which all data is contained in one table.

Information Architecture is a description or design specification for how information should be treated and organized.

Information Sharing occurs in organizations that encourage sharing information and use collaboration, mentoring, and socialization to inform people.

Instruction is information that is taught. When a learning need requires instruction, training is provided. Instruction may include information incorporating corporate ideals, expectations, safety, and related materials and can be delivered via classroom instruction, e-learning, and on-the-job training.

IPO (Input/Process/Output) refers to systems used to transform data and information. Examples include technological innovations such as voice and handwriting recognition systems and computer touch pads. As interventions, these systems help individuals improve their performance by enabling and empowering them through the use of devices that facilitate and adapt work processes to individual needs and preferences.

Intervention is another name for a solution or set of solutions, usually a combination of tools and techniques that clearly and directly relate to solving a performance gap.

Knowledge Audits clarify the type of information employees need and highlight any barriers to sharing organizational knowledge.

Knowledge Base is the capturing and storing of data and information in a central or distributed electronic environment.

Knowledge Exchanges, also known as knowledge exchange networks, enable different groups in an organization to share documents and information on products to create lists of links in simple webpages and to discuss issues of mutual interest.

Knowledge Management (KM) is the explicit and systematic management of intellectual capital and organization knowledge as well as the associated processes of creating, gathering, organizing, disseminating, leveraging, and using intellectual capital for the purposes of improvement of the organization and the individual within the organization.

Knowledge Mapping is a process that connects information, education expertise, and practical application of people in the organization for the purposes of sharing and access.

Knowledge Repository is a category of technology that offers products for creating, storing, and managing a corporate knowledge.

Knowledge Spiral displays the interaction between tacit and explicit knowledge.

Knowledge Survey is a tool used to collect the types of information that employees have, as well as information they need to do their jobs.

Learning Style describes an individual's approach to learning that involves the way he or she behaves, feels, and processes information.

MDBs (Multidimensional Databases) are often generated from relational databases and designed to optimize analytical processing.

Pedagogy is an informal philosophy of teaching that focuses on what the instructor does rather than what the participants learn. Usually references the teaching of children.

Process Map is a visual tool used to systematically describe actions and behaviors in a sequential flow.

Project Life Cycle is everything that happens from the beginning to the end of the project.

RDBMS (Relational Database Management System) stores data in the form of tables linked by a unique identifier.

Six Sigma Methodology is a process-improvement strategy and measure of quality that strives for near perfection. Six Sigma is a disciplined, data-driven methodology for eliminating defects (driving toward six standard deviations between the mean and the nearest specification limit) in a process. The fundamental objective of the Six Sigma methodology is the implementation of a measurement-based strategy that focuses on process improvement and variation reduction through the application of projects.

Snowball Sample means that when one employee mentions resources and people who have knowledge, researchers talk with those employees, find more resource names and information, and so on.

Strategic Planning is the process that allows an organization to identify its aspirations and future challenges, clarify and gain consensus around a business strategy, communicate the strategy throughout the organization, align departments and personal goals with the overarching organizational strategy, and identify and align strategic initiatives. Often combined with long-term (five to ten year) planning initiatives, the process typically involves a SWOT analysis.

Surveys collect the type of information employees have as well as the type of information they need to do their jobs.

SWOT (Strengths, Weakness, Opportunities, and Threats) is an analysis tool used in strategic planning to establish environmental factors from within and outside an organization.

System Development Life Cycle is an organizational process of developing and maintaining systems. It helps in establishing a system project plan and lists the processes and subprocesses required to develop a system.

System Tests are conducted with real data. If the outputs of the test don't match the specifications, errors are identified and corrected.

Tacit is a type of knowledge refers to personal knowledge in one's head—knowing how to do something based on experience.

Unit Tests are conducted in real working conditions using test data. Any errors must be noted and corrected.

WBT (Web-Based Training) refers to the delivery of educational content via a Web browser over the Internet, a private intranet, or an extranet.

Web Portals are sites on the World Wide Web that typically provide personalized capabilities to their visitors.

Appendix B Answer Key

Chapter 1

1. Knowledge management is the explicit and systematic management of intellectual capital and is concerned with turning explicit knowledge into tacit knowledge.

B. False

The statement is false. Although knowledge management is in fact the explicit and systematic management of intellectual capital—as well as the associated processes of creating, gathering, organizing, retrieving, leveraging, and using intellectual capital for the purposes of improving organizations and the people in them—knowledge management does not concern itself with turning explicit knowledge into tacit knowledge. It is concerned with the exact opposite: turning tacit knowledge—or individual know-how—into explicit knowledge, in the form of documented information, processes, and steps.

2. Which type of knowledge refers to personal knowledge in one's head, or knowing how to do something based on experience? It includes judgment, insights, experience, know-how, personal beliefs, and values.

B. Tacit

Response B is correct because tacit knowledge refers to something that an employee knows or is able to do without having to refer to any other documentation, such as a training manual. It is simply knowledge that has been learned from experience.

3. A WLP professional is conducting a study on the effects of a training program she is delivering. She is drawing on her own experiences to guide the study. What type of knowledge is being represented by the professional?

B. Tacit

Response B is correct because tacit knowledge refers to knowledge that one has in one's head that is based on personal experience. In the example, the WLP professional is thinking back to her own experiences and thus the knowledge she is using is tacit.

4. All the following are elements of knowledge management *except*

A. Classroom instruction

Response A is correct because knowledge management uses information sharing rather than instruction, which is information that is taught. Classroom instruction is not one of the elements of knowledge management.

5. Which best describes a central or distributed environment in which an organization captures and stores data?

D. Knowledge base

Response D is correct because a knowledge base houses knowledge that has been gathered from people in the organization; frequently it includes tacit knowledge that has been made explicit through documentation.

6. Instruction is information that is shared formally or informally.

B. False

The statement is false because instruction is information that is formally taught and can be delivered through classroom instruction, e-learning, and on-the-job training.

7. Which type of knowledge includes information that has been documented or can be shared with someone else?

A. Explicit

Response A is correct because explicit knowledge refers to knowledge that has been documented in some form.

8. Which of the following best describes the key goal of knowledge management?

B. To effectively share knowledge throughout an organization for the benefit of the organization or the individual

Response B is correct because knowledge management enables knowledge to be disseminated across an organization so that employees have access to information they need to work smarter and contribute to organizational goals.

9. A trainer is working with a team of specialists who require a collaborative information-sharing environment to help them stay up to date on the latest technology advancements. Based on this information, what can be said about this group and knowledge management?

A. The collaborative requirements align with the goals of knowledge management

Response A is correct because collaboration is one of the key elements of knowledge management.

10. In building an effective knowledge management system, a training manager begins to construct a web management tool to allow employees to access vital and timely information from anywhere. He then takes prerecorded messages from the president of the company and places the clips on the site for employees to also view at their leisure. Next, he looks to extend the balance of the offering by

C. Creating a collaboration area for people to meet and discuss ideas with others in the company

Response C is correct because a key element of knowledge management is the ability to connect with other people around the organization to collaborate and learn from one another.

Chapter 2

1. All of the following contributed to the history of knowledge management *except*

B. Structured compensation systems

Response B is correct because structured compensation systems did not contribute to the development of knowledge management. Compensation is a function of HR that is unrelated to learning and information sharing.

2. Knowledge can be viewed as an object and as a process.

A. True

The statement is true because many theorists discuss knowledge from two perspectives: as an object and as a process. Exemplifying the perspective of knowledge as a object is the fact that many types of learning content management systems use the term "knowledge objects" to define the pieces of content that may be used to build a course. However, from the perspective of knowledge as a process, knowledge can be used to assess, change, and improve human skills and behavior. Ultimately, the focus is to make

knowledge available when it's needed to change human behavior.

3. A trainer is learning about the origin of knowledge management. Which of the following statements is *not* a fact about the beginnings of the concept?

C. Peter Drucker is considered to be "the father of knowledge management" because of his work in the area

Response C is correct because Peter Drucker is not considered "the father of knowledge management"; he is one of many contributors to the history of knowledge management, as are Karl-Erik Sveiby and Peter Senge.

4. Collaboration involves two or more people, departments, and companies working together for the success of the organization's people, processes, and future livelihood.

A. True

The statement is true because collaboration is a best practice that has people working together for the good of the organization by focusing on dialogue and interaction to learn more, generate ideas, and share knowledge.

5. Which of the following is *not* an example of best practices for knowledge management in an organization?

C. Explicit knowledge

Response C is correct because explicit knowledge is not a best practice; it is a type of knowledge that is captured through documentation.

6. Which of the following best describes how measurement is used to improve best practices?

A. The goal of best practice is continuous improvement, and without measurement, there's no benchmark to know whether processes and metrics are improving.

Response A is correct because best practices, also referred to as best of breed, are techniques that are believed to constitute a paradigm of excellence in a particular field. Therefore, the goal of using them is to identify what the best looks like to make improvements and have a benchmark to measure progress against.

7. A trainer is looking at several knowledge management best practices. Which of the following is *not* considered a best practice in knowledge management?

D. Managing

Response D is correct because managing is not a best practice in knowledge management. It is a behavior that is applicable to many areas of an organization.

8. A WLP professional is creating short reference materials containing codified, categorized, reusable content to enable people to quickly find and easily understand the information. What best practice does this activity refer to?

C. Information chunking

Response C is correct because information chunking involves creating logical and convenient information documented in an easy-to-use format, such as a table or a text box.

Chapter 3

1. Which of the following best describes knowledge mapping?

C. A process that identifies the location, ownership, value, and use of information and knowledge.

Response C is correct because knowledge mapping identifies an organization's experts, best communicators, and best practices in an effort to clarify information in an organization.

2. Some types of knowledge include tacit and explicit, formal and informal, and short and imperative.

B. False

The statement is false because "short and imperative" is a not a form of knowledge. Types of knowledge include tacit and explicit, formal and informal, codified and personalized, internal and external, and short life cycle or permanent.

3. A training manager is trying to conduct a knowledge survey to determine the origin of a vital training exercise. As she works with one of the founding partners, she discovers some information that refers her to several persons and other documents detailing vital pieces of information that make up this knowledge base. Based on the information above, this is an example of snowball sampling.

A. True

The statement is true because snowball sampling means that while a researcher is looking for information, he or she may talk to an employee who mentions resources and people with knowledge, researchers then talk with those employees, find more resource names and information, and so on. In the example, the training manager discovers s everal more people and documents after talking with one of the founding partners, which exemplifies a snowball sample.

4. Corporate culture does not have an effect on knowledge management in an organization.

B. False

The statement is false because corporate culture has a powerful effect on knowledge management. All organizations are different in size, specialization, organization structure, communication, and so forth. These differences have a great effect on how knowledge is collected, stored, and shared.

5. The attitude of management can help or hinder knowledge management in an organization.

A. True

The statement is true because any negative attitudes that management may have—such as viewing use of the knowledge management system as surfing or wasting time—will discourage employees from using the system. Alternatively, providing people with the time to look for information they need and encouraging people to use the system will help the use of knowledge management in an organization.

6. A training manager is constructing an incentive plan for encouraging behavioral change. The behaviors being targeted link directly to a new collaborative tool that is being promoted internally to help facilitate virtual meetings. This description is an example of implementing an incentive program in support of knowledge management.

A. True

The statement is true because the example shows a training manager trying to create an environment and culture where knowledge sharing is encouraged through incentives.

7. All of the following are all examples of ways to capture knowledge in an organization *except*

C. Conducting performance reviews

Response C is correct because a performance review is a confidential conversation between an employee and his or her manager and is not appropriate as a means of capturing knowledge to be shared across an organization.

8. The following are all examples of ways to establish support for knowledge management in an organization *except*

C. Selecting the most advanced technology available

Response C is correct because it's important to be selective about the technology used when starting a knowledge management initiative. The most advanced technology available may not be appropriate for an organization for a number of reasons, including incompatibility with the existing information technology infrastructure and the culture.

9. Organizations often see an improvement in the introduction and implementation of metrics after instituting knowledge management.

A. True

The statement is true because setting target metrics is a way to link task output to organizational goals, while process reviews and lessons learned are gathered and added to a knowledge repository to be accessed for future use.

Chapter 5

1. Which of the following types of analysis attempts to standardize workflow in a manner that decreases redundancy of effort and increases information reuse?

A. Business process analysis

Response A is correct because business process analysis is a structured method of documenting business rules and uncovers hidden inefficiencies and strengths that could be streamlined or leveraged to increase productivity.

2. A WLP professional is beginning a new major project. What should be the first step in this or any other major project?

B. Analyze and define the business processes

Response B is correct because business process analysis is a prerequisite for any new project to analyze and define how people, materials, methods, machines, and the environment combine to add value to a product or service and communicate relevant information to employees.

3. A WLP professional is constructing a process map that will be used to communicate the project to management. A process map is most typically used to

A. Pinpoint the problem areas and opportunities for improvement

Response A is correct because a process map presents a clear and logical visual representation of all the tasks and steps involved in carrying out a particular process, which allows the WLP professional to identify potential bottlenecks or problems, and prevent them from interrupting the process.

4. Which of the following is a visual tool used to systematically describe actions and behaviors in a sequential flow?

B. Process map

Response B is correct because a process map presents a clear and logical visual representation of all the tasks and steps involved in carrying out a particular process.

5. All of the following area examples of risk analysis and contingency planning *except*

B. A group of line workers discusses the new labor relations contract and the effect of the contract on overtime pay.

Response B is correct because discussing a new labor relations contract and its effect on overtime pay is not a way to identify potential barriers to a project and plan a way to avoid or get around the barrier.

6. Six Sigma is a business-driven approach to improvement that seeks to improve customer satisfaction by providing more effective sales and product training for the sales force.

B. False

The statement is false because Six Sigma focuses on improving customer satisfaction by reducing defects.

7. Because all organizations are composed of systems that interact with each other, which of the following tools focuses on the main components of any system including people, products or services, and processes?

D. Six Sigma IPO model

Response D is correct because process thinking is the linchpin of Six Sigma, making processes another focus of the Six Sigma methodology. The IPO model depicts the input, the process or action taken on the input, and the outcome or result of the action.

8. The project lifecycle is everything that happens from the beginning to the end of the project, and includes the analysis, design, development, implementation, and evaluation phases on every project.

B. False

The statement is false because although the project lifecycle does include everything that happens from the beginning to the end of the project, it does not include analysis, design, development, implementation, and evaluation phases. These elements comprise the ADDIE model of designing and developing learning.

9. A project manager's focus should be on

C. Scope , time, cost, quality, and resource use

Response C is correct because the job of the project manager is to plan, organize, and manage project tasks, based on the elements of time, money, and available resources.

10. A WLP professional has just constructed a 452-task project plan complete with dates and phases. Why has she chosen to incorporate phases into her project plan?

A. To focus energy on current work with the ability to look ahead

Response A is correct because using phases enables a project manager to divide project work into manageable chunks. Then, the project manager can focus on current work and anticipate upcoming work, without becoming overwhelmed by the overall scope of the project.

Chapter 6

1. Which of the following systems manages components that make up a course?

B. LCMS

Response B is correct because in an LCMS, content is chunked (typically into learning objects, which are small, reusable pieces of content) and then managed, published, and delivered on demand.

2. A training manager is attempting to provide a tool that will allow employees to readily access small chunks of learning quickly and as frequently as needed. Which management system will best meet the training manager's needs?

B. LCMS

Response B is correct because in an LCMS, content is chunked (typically into learning objects, which are small, reusable pieces of content) and then managed, published, and delivered on demand.

3. A training manager is working to deploy a series of PDFs and other critical information so that they are readily accessible to employees. Which management system best represents the needed solution?

C. CMS

Response C is correct because a CMS can publish content to multiple formats, including HTML (web), printed, PDF, and hand-held.

4. A training manager is working through the phases of content management. Which of the following is *not* considered a phase in the lifecycle of a content management system?

D. Execution

Response D is correct because execution is not one of the phases of content management.

5. Which of the content management process phases helps to provide disaster recovery capabilities?

B. Content management

Response B is correct because content management enables version control, which allows only one version of a document to be updated at a time and provides legal accountability, backup, and disaster recovery capabilities.

6. Which of the following includes email, computer networks, whiteboards, bulletin board systems, chat rooms, and online presentation tools, which play an important role in the expansion of e-learning and in collaborating on projects, sharing information, and communicating?

D. Collaboration tools

Response D is correct because knowledge-sharing products, such as email, computer networks, and whiteboards help with collecting and exchanging organizational information.

7. A trainer has accessed her company's training site to make content additions and tweak user information. She has been enabled to do so by accessing

B. A portal

Response B is correct because an enterprise portal offers services that support the full life cycle of document creation and provide mechanisms for authoring, approval, version control, scheduled publishing, indexing, and searching.

8. A WLP professional is beginning work on a Six Sigma project and needs to access content specific to this topic. She enters her company's knowledge management intranet site and subscribes to several services that can continue to keep her updated on the topic. Which portal feature has she just benefited from?

C. Personalization

Response C is correct because personalization allows portal members to subscribe to specific types of content and services. Users can also customize the look and feel of their environment.

9. Document management systems accomplish all of the following *except*

D. Editing

Response D is correct because document management systems do not allow editing. They are used to track and store documents.

10. A training manager is trying to retain information from old documents so that project teams have access to the legacy information. Which type of management system best meets this need?

C. Document

Response C is correct because a document management system enables an organization to track and store documents.

Chapter 7

1. A WLP professional is reviewing the information architecture for a system being built. The specifications include the mission and vision of the site and a description of how learners will access the system. The specifications also include the plan for navigation and search functions. The piece of the information architecture that appears to be missing is the type of RDBMS that will be used.

B. False

The statement is false because information architecture focuses on defining the mission and vision for the site; determining what content and functionality are needed for the site; and identifying how learners will access information by defining organization, navigation, labeling, and search capabilities. The information architecture described in the question provides the mission, vision, and learner access, including navigation and search functions, but not what content and functionality are needed. An RDBMS, or relational database management system, stores data in the form of tables linked by a unique identifier.

2. Collaborative communication is a critical part of a good personal knowledge management strategy.

A. True

The statement is true because sharing information and knowledge can lead to new ideas and knowledge to add value to an organization. A knowledge management system should include plenty of opportunities for people to interact with each other through discussion groups, email, instant messaging, communities of practice or knowledge exchanges, and so forth.

3. A training manager has pulled information from the knowledge management system that describes copyright information and keywords for search engines. What information is he likely looking at?

B. Metatag

Response B is correct because a metatag is an HTML tag identifying the contents of information on a website or in a knowledge base. Information commonly found in a metatag includes copyright information, keywords for search engines, and page formatting descriptions.

4. A training manager is reviewing the key considerations when using collaboration to support knowledge management. Which of the following is *not* a key consideration?

D. The competitive landscape and how this tool can be compromised

Response D is correct because the competitive landscape and how the tool can be compromised is not a key consideration of using collaboration to support knowledge management.

5. Which of the following is best described as a system to help employees access and share information to solve problems and grow the collective knowledge of the organization?

A. Knowledge base

Response A is correct because a knowledge base organizes data and information so that workers can quickly enter and retrieve information, providing easy access and sharing capabilities.

6. Which of the following is an HTML tag that includes copyright information, keywords for search engines, and page formatting descriptions?

B. Metatag

Response B is correct because a metatag is an HTML tag identifying the contents of information on a website or in a knowledge base, such as copyright information, keywords for search engines, and page formatting descriptions.

7. When implementing a knowledge management system, all of the following are key considerations regarding the nature and collection of knowledge *except*

D. Cost

Response D is correct because cost is not a factor that relates to the nature and collection of knowledge.

8. A WLP professional is working with her IT department to make certain that the sales management tool the client is using is effective and user friendly. What is the most important factor she should ensure about the tool?

A. Easy to access

Response A is correct because the organization of information in any kind of knowledge base, including a sales management tool, should make the level of detail in the knowledge base easy to discern and

navigate. If users can't understand the information and how to easily access it, they won't use it.

9. A training manager is looking for a design specification on how the new knowledge management system will be constructed and how the data will be organized in the system. What term best describes what the manager is looking for?

C. Information architecture

Response C is correct because information architecture is a description or design specification for how information should be treated and organized. In web design, the term describes organizing online content into categories and creating an interface for displaying those categories.

10. A training manager is reviewing several ways to capture information for a system architecture project. She notices that each week a group of project leads meet to discuss their projects and exchange ideas. The concept seems perfect for her project and so she decides to create the same type of group for her project. This type of strategy can best be considered as what type of knowledge capturing?

B. Collaboration

Response B is correct because collaboration refers to sharing information and knowledge that can lead to the creation of new ideas and knowledge to add value to an organization.

Chapter 8

1. The purpose of a DBMS is to provide a storage mechanism that can support efficient storage and retrieval of large amounts of data.

A. True

The statement is true because a DBMS is a collection of programs enabling the efficient storage and retrieval of large amounts of data.

2. Databases offer all of the following features *except*

C. Ability to share information and knowledge, leading to the creation of new ideas and new knowledge

Response C is correct because the ability to share information and knowledge to create new ideas

and knowledge is a feature of collaboration tools, not of databases.

3. What kind of database makes it easy to work with individual records for updating, but also enables users to view database information in many different ways?

A. Relational database

Response A is correct because relational databases store data in the form of tables linked by a unique identifier. These relationships provide the power behind RDBMSs because they require few assumptions as to how data is linked and related.

4. Many database installations may use a combination of two databases, for example relational and multidimensional.

A. True

The statement is true because some database installations store detailed data in a relational database and use a multidimensional database for certain data marts with well-known analysis patterns.

5. A training manager is requiring that the database back end to his learning management system be very powerful and able to link data across several tables of information about courses, resources, and employees taking training. What would be the best type of database to support this type of application?

B. Relational

Response B is correct because a relational database allows the user to store data in many different tables and view the database information in many different ways.

6. The questions that individuals can pose when searching a database take the form of search statements.

B. False

The statement is false because the questions that individuals can pose when searching a database take the form of queries, another name for a tool that asks a question of a database.

7. A training manager is looking to house a collection of tools and systems that play a role in strategic planning to help the training unit make decisions. What type of tool is the training manager looking for?

A. Business intelligence tools

Response A is correct because business intelligence tools are the tools and systems that play a role in strategic planning to help organizations make decisions and determine how a training initiative can have the strongest impact. The properties of these tools often include sophisticated optimization, query parallelism, mechanisms to partition large tables, and resource governors.

8. Performance testing for a knowledge management system is important because in any system implementation there are going to be unexpected performance problems that must be tested before the system "goes live."

A. True

The statement is true because all IT implementations are complicated, and performance testing allows experts to plan for unanticipated issues. It's not unusual to have a lengthy prototype testing timeline to deal with unexpected performance problems, such as workload and process optimization.

9. A WLP professional has been alerted to large files requiring organizing in the database management system. What support is likely needed for this issue?

C. Analysis of unstructured objects

Response C is correct because when a DBMS includes large objects such as text and other information, IT professionals need to analyze these unstructured objects to determine how to manage and store them and to establish processes for controlling how the computer collects and analyzes data.

10. A WLP professional is attempting to pull together a resource team to support the implementation of the knowledge management system. Which of the following factors is *not* considered part of an RDBMS?

D. Flat file creations

Response D is correct because an RDBMS uses a relational database and not a flat file database, therefore flat file creations are not a part of an RDBMS.

Chapter 9

1. One technique used to map work process flow includes the input-analysis-output model.

B. False

The statement is false because the technique to map work process flow is the input-process-output (IPO) model, which refers to systems for transforming data and information, and depicts an input, the process or action taken on the input, and the outcome or result of the action.

2. All of the following are standard phases in a system development life cycle *except*

C. Communication

Response C is correct because communication is not a standard phase in a system development life cycle, which is an organizational process of developing and maintaining systems.

3. Each phase of a project has one primary deliverable.

B. False

The statement is false because the various phases of a project can have more than one deliverable.

4. The testing phase of a systems implementation often includes two types—one with test data and one with real data.

A. True

The statement is true because two types of tests may be run during the testing phase of a systems implementation. Unit tests are conducted in real working conditions using test data. Any errors must be noted and corrected. System tests are conducted with real data. If the outputs of the test don't match the specifications, errors are identified and corrected.

5. Which of the following systems implementation phases requires converting the blueprint of the system into computer programming language?

B. Coding

Response B is correct because during the coding phase of systems implementation, the defined procedures in the documentation are translated into control specifications and computer instructions to indicate data movement and control of the entire system.

6. The IPO model functions within a project management framework

A. True

The statement is true because the IPO model functions within a project management framework to

plan and assign the work to be accomplished on time, within budget, and within scope.

7. A WLP professional is working with the software creation team and has been notified that the team is in the coding stage of the cycle. Based on your knowledge of how system development works, what stage in the cycle happens next?

A. Implementation

Response A is correct because implementation takes place after testing and user acceptance. The system is installed on user computers and training ensues, based on learning objectives.

8. Collectively, all phases of a project are known as the

C. Project life cycle

Response C is correct because all tasks from the beginning to the end of a project is called the project life cycle.

9. The maintenance phase focuses on eliminating errors in the system and to identify and reduce variations.

A. True

The statement is true because maintenance is an ongoing process to correct errors and to identify and reduce any variations in system output compared to the specifications.

Chapter 12

1. Which of the following best describes why measuring an organization's knowledge management initiative is important?

C. Measurement is the only way an organization, a department, or a person can assess outcomes or potential improvement.

Response C, which indicates that measurement is the only way an organization, a department, or a person can assess outcomes or potential improvement, is correct because analyzing the actions that occurred becomes a learning process and a way to capture issues, identify problems, and document successful solutions.

2. The purpose of after action reviews in many organizations is to continually identify which content needs to be updated in the knowledge management system.

B. False

The statement is false because the purpose of after action reviews is to ensure people learn from their experiences.

3. After action reviews use a series of questions to facilitate the discussion and review process.

A. True

The statement is true because after action reviews use a process of five questions to enable teams and individuals to analyze what happened during the project: What was the intent? What happened? What was learned? What does the group or person do now? Who else should be told?

4. Which of the following terms describes the type of information captured that may have been used to solve problems, discover how mishaps were prevented, or recognize opportunities?

D. Lessons learned

Response D is correct because lessons learned refers to information that employees involved in the project uncovered during its course; examples of lessons learned are solved problems, how a mishap was prevented, a recognized opportunity, and so on.

5. AARs were first conducted by the U.S. Army as a structured way to get people to capture their learning and experiences.

A. True

The statement is true because the U.S. Army was the first large entity to use AARs to identify the original intent of a mission, what went right and wrong, and what factors affected the mission and the situations presented.

6. An AAR is one formal method of

D. Knowledge management

Response D is correct because AARs are a way to capture lessons learned about a project by identifying problems, identifying possible solutions and people involved, initiating a plan for knowledge sharing, and evaluating success.

7. A training manager is selling his management team on using AARs for their key projects. The management team thinks it is a waste of time and resources to do this task. What key point would be helpful to persuade the management team to conduct AARs in the future?

A. The identification of lessons learned can help other groups save time

Response A is correct because AARs enable organizations to capture lessons learned from projects and to disseminate that information to others who may need it on similar projects in the future.

Appendix C
Index

**ASTD Learning System
Editorial Staff**

Director: Cat Russo
Manager: Mark Morrow
Editors: Tora Estep, Jennifer
Mitchell

Contributing Editors

April Davis, Stephanie Sussan

Proofreading

April Davis, Eva Kaplan-Leiserson

Graphic Design

Kathleen Schaner

Indexer

April Davis

Thomson NETg Staff

Solutions Manager: Robyn Rickenbach
Director: John Pydyn

Contributing Writers

Lynn Lewis, Dawn Rader

Editors

Lisa Lord, Kim Lindros, Karen Day

ASTD (American Society for Training & Development) is the world's largest association dedicated to workplace learning and performance professionals. ASTD's 70,000 members and associates come from more than 100 countries and thousands of organizations--multinational corporations, medium-sized and small businesses, government, academia, consulting firms, and product and service suppliers.

ASTD marks its beginning in 1944 when the organization held its first annual conference. In recent years, ASTD has widened the industry's focus to connect learning and performance to measurable results, and is a sought-after voice on critical public policy issues.

Thomson NETg, formerly backed by The Thomson Corporation, was a global enterprise comprised of a vast array of world-renowned publishing and information assets in the areas of academics, business and government, financial services, science and health care, and the law. NETg was acquired by SkillSoft in 2007.